THE IMPORTANCE OF

Golda Meir

These and other titles are included in The Importance Of biography series:

THE IMPORTANCE OF

Golda Meir

by
Deborah Hitzeroth

Lucent Books, P.O. Box 289011, San Diego, CA 92198-9011

Library of Congress Cataloging-in-Publication Data

Hitzeroth, Deborah, 1961–
    The importance of Golda Meir / by Deborah Hitzeroth.
      p.   cm.—(The importance of)
    Includes bibliographical references and index.
    Summary: A biography of the woman who dedicated her
life to the creation and preservation of a Jewish state.
    ISBN 1-56006-090-5 (lib. bdg. : alk. paper)
    1. Meir, Golda, 1898–1978—Juvenile literature.
2. Women prime ministers—Israel—Biography—Juvenile
literature.   [1. Meir, Golda, 1898–1978.   2. Prime ministers.
3. Women—Biography.]   I. Title.   II. Series.
DS126.M42H58   1998
956.9405'3'092—dc21   97–36465
[B]   CIP
                                  AC

Copyright 1998 by Lucent Books, Inc., P.O. Box 289011,
San Diego, California 92198-9011

Printed in the U.S.A.

Contents

Foreword

THE IMPORTANCE OF biography series deals with individuals who have made a unique contribution to history. The editors of the series have deliberately chosen to cast a wide net and include people from all fields of endeavor. Individuals from politics, music, art, literature, philosophy, science, sports, and religion are all represented. In addition, the editors did not restrict the series to individuals whose accomplishments have helped change the course of history. Of necessity, this criterion would have eliminated many whose contribution was great, though limited. Charles Darwin, for example, was responsible for radically altering the scientific view of the natural history of the world. His achievements continue to impact the study of science today. Others, such as Chief Joseph of the Nez Percé, played a pivotal role in the history of their own people. While Joseph's influence does not extend much beyond the Nez Percé, his nonviolent resistance to white expansion and his continuing role in protecting his tribe and his homeland remain an inspiration to all.

These biographies are more than factual chronicles. Each volume attempts to emphasize an individual's contributions both in his or her own time and for posterity. For example, the voyages of Christopher Columbus opened the way to European colonization of the New World. Unquestionably, his encounter with the New World brought monumental changes to both Europe and the Americas in his day. Today, however, the broader impact of Columbus's voyages is being critically scrutinized. *Christopher Columbus,* as well as every biography in The Importance Of series, includes and evaluates the most recent scholarship available on each subject.

Each author includes a wide variety of primary and secondary source quotations to document and substantiate his or her work. All quotes are footnoted to show readers exactly how and where biographers derive their information, as well as provide stepping stones to further research. These quotations enliven the text by giving readers eyewitness views of the life and times of each individual covered in The Importance Of series.

Finally, each volume is enhanced by photographs, bibliographies, chronologies, and comprehensive indexes. For both the casual reader and the student engaged in research, The Importance Of biographies will be a fascinating adventure into the lives of people who have helped shape humanity's past and present, and who will continue to shape its future.

IMPORTANT DATES IN THE LIFE OF GOLDA MEIR

1898
Golda Mabovits is born May 3 in Kiev, Ukraine.

1903
Golda's father, Moshe, leaves for the United States.

1906
Golda, her two sisters, and her mother immigrate to America.

1909
Performs first "public work" and holds a fund-raiser for students who cannot afford books.

1917
Balfour Declaration, announcing Britain's support for a Jewish homeland, is issued; Golda and Morris Meyerson marry and pledge to immigrate to Palestine.

1921
Golda and Morris immigrate to Palestine, join Kibbutz Merhavia.

1927
Becomes secretary of the Women's Labor Council of the Histadrut, or Jewish Labor Federation.

1935
Becomes a member of the Vaad Hapoel's steering committee.

1948
State of Israel is created May 15; Meir is one of thirty-seven people to sign the new nation's Declaration of Independence; becomes first Israeli ambassador to Russia.

1949
David Ben-Gurion is elected as Israel's first prime minister; he appoints Meir minister of labor.

1956
Becomes Israeli foreign minister.

1958
Develops farming and educational programs to help emerging African nations and makes first tour of Africa.

1966
Leaves office to spend more time with her family but is named leader of the Mapai Party, one of the leading political parties in Israel.

1967
Israel engages the armies of Egypt, Syria, and Jordan in the Six-Day War.

1968
Mapai Party merges with other social-democratic political parties to become the Israel Labor Party.

1969
Prime Minister Levi Eshkol dies; Meir is named acting prime minister and then elected prime minister.

1973
Yom Kippur War catches Israel by surprise, resulting in heavy losses.

1974
Resigns from office.

1978
Dies at age eighty after a fifteen-year battle with cancer.

1979
Egypt and Israel sign peace treaty.

1993
Leaders of Israel and Palestine Liberation Organization sign a peace accord.

1994
Jordan and Israel sign treaty officially ending forty-six-year state of war.

A Woman of Deep Convictions

Golda Meir did not plan to lead the kind of life that would win her a place in history books. Though her dreams were large, they were not filled with thoughts of wealth or fame for herself. Instead she dreamed of a homeland for the Jewish people—a place where they could control their own destiny and live free of persecution. She saw her role in the building of the homeland as simply that of any settler who helped build a new nation. In her autobiography, Meir wrote:

> I had never planned to be prime minister; I had never planned any position in fact. I had planned to [go] to Palestine, to go to [a kibbutz], to be active in the labor movement. But the position I would occupy? That never.[1]

Committed to the Struggle

Meir committed her life to the struggle for a Jewish nation, and in the course of the struggle she lived a life filled with heroic and dangerous deeds. She faced imprisonment to help smuggle refugees escaping from World War II Europe into Palestine, and she faced gunfire from opponents to the creation of Israel. And though she never aspired to fame, her work brought her international recognition and won her a place in history. Meir was the first Israeli ambassador to Russia, the country's first minister of labor, the first female foreign minister, and the first female prime minister of a Middle Eastern country.

Golda Meir played a pivotal role in Israel's history—in the beginning she raised funds for settlers, but she later became the nation's prime minister.

From her childhood she developed an iron will and adopted the view that if one believed in something, he or she must take action and personal responsibility to make the belief a reality. Meir found that action often meant sacrifice and loss, but throughout her life she accepted the price of following her dreams:

> Anybody who believes in something without reservation, believes that this thing is right and should be, has the stamina to meet obstacles and overcome them. . . . From my early youth I believed in two things: one, the need for Jewish sovereignty, so that Jews—and this has become a cliché—can be the master of their own fate; and two, [in] a society based on justice and equality, without exploitation. But I was never so naive or foolish to think that if you merely believe in something it happens. You must struggle for it.[2]

This is the story of Meir's life and her struggle to create a Jewish homeland.

1 The Shaping of a Revolutionary

As an adult looking back on her life, Golda Meir remembered a childhood fraught with fear, hunger, and powerlessness. Memories of seeing friends beaten and dragged from their homes, of living in constant fear that soldiers would come for her and her family, haunted Meir throughout her life. These experiences shaped her iron will and made her into the woman who would one day help guide a struggling new nation to independence.

In her autobiography, Meir described the effects of her childhood in early-twentieth-century Russia:

> My early childhood in Russia . . . sums up my beginnings. . . . I have very few happy or even pleasant memories of this time. The isolated episodes that have stayed with me . . . have to do mostly with the terrible hardships my family suffered, with poverty, cold, hunger and fear, and I suppose my recollection of being frightened is the clearest of all my memories.[3]

The Eve of Revolution

Golda's family suffered because they were different—they were Jews. The Jewish peo-ple are the descendants of an ancient peo-ple called the Hebrews whose history dates back more than thirty-five hundred years. The religion and culture of the Jews is called Judaism. It is today one of the world's major religions and was the first to teach the belief in one god, or monotheism, rather than the prevailing belief in many gods, or pantheism.

The beliefs of the Jewish faith are outlined in two books, the Torah and the Talmud. These two books contain the basic laws of Judaism and serve as the foundation of civil and religious laws for the Jewish faith. The books also dictate many of the daily customs of the Jewish people, including the types of food they eat and the way they dress. Following these traditions set Jewish families apart from most citizens of the Russian Empire, and being different was dangerous. During the early 1900s it was safer to blend in than to attract the attention of the government.

The Russian Empire was undergoing violent changes in the late 1800s and early 1900s. The country was suffering from periodic famines, and the economy was unstable. Workers were forming unions and striking to pressure the government into providing better working conditions. At the time, hours were long, pay was low, and factory conditions were dangerous. Some

Russification

Tsar Nicholas II of Russia reigned during a time of turmoil and revolution. In an effort to unify his country, Nicholas implemented a program of Russification.

workers even advocated the violent overthrow of the Russian monarchy, headed by Tsar Nicholas II. A Russian tsar was the equivalent of a king, and Nicholas had absolute power over the country. Many workers felt that Nicholas was abusing his power and was not helping his people.

In an effort to counter stirrings of rebellion, Nicholas developed a plan to mold the diverse population of his huge empire into a single people who would share political and religious beliefs. Nicholas believed that a national identity would build loyalty to his government and erase the desire for revolt. To do this, Nicholas instituted a policy he called Russification.

Through a series of harsh laws and tyrannical actions, Nicholas tried to force all the peoples of the Russian empire to conform to his idea of a unified Russia. Nicholas's government censored all publications that did not support his views and imposed harsh penalties on anyone who did not obey his mandates. Those who disobeyed were subject to beatings and torture. As part of the Russification program, Nicholas also tried to force everyone to convert to the Russian Orthodox faith. The Russian Orthodox Church had a long history of supporting the tsar's policies. In turn, Nicholas supported the church and endorsed it as the official church of Russia. Under the Russification policy, religious persecution grew and those who did not belong to the official church were pressured to convert. The Jewish people, many of whom refused to embrace the Russian Orthodox faith, became one of Nicholas's main targets. The Jews who clung to their traditional dress and religious customs were an easily discernible target because they looked and acted different from their neighbors. Russian Jews suffered greatly under the new policy.

During Nicholas's reign six hundred laws were passed regarding the Jewish population. These laws governed everything from where a Jew could live to when and whether a Jewish couple could marry. The state even decided how many Jewish marriages could take place each year. Russian law also prohibited Jews from living anywhere but in the "Pale of Jewish Settlement."

The Jewish Pale was an area in western Russia that had formerly been part of Poland and was already home to a large

Jewish population. The term *pale* means an area enclosed by a fence or boundary and is often used to describe an area where one race of people lives under the control of another race or nationality. By using this term to describe the Jewish settlement, the Russian government was branding the Jews as outsiders.

Though Nicholas continued to make harsher and harsher laws to control his subjects, the Russification program failed to stem the rebellion. In desperation, Nicholas tried to deflect anger from his government to another target. The Jews were that target. Nicholas publicly blamed Russia's economic and other problems on the Jewish population. His advisers did the same. Rumors spread that Russian Jews were getting rich while most Russian workers could barely feed their families. Other rumors blamed the growing cost of food and clothing on Jewish merchants who wanted to increase their profits.

The rumors led to violence by Russians against the Jewish people. In cities throughout the empire, Jewish people were attacked by mobs, and many were beaten to death. The local authorities did little to stop these outbreaks, called pogroms, and in some areas even encouraged them.

Growing Up in a Troubled World

This is the world into which Golda Mabovits was born on May 3, 1898. Her birthplace was Kiev, in the Russian Ukraine. Her family was poor and her parents, Moshe and Blume, had to struggle to care for the family. Moshe was a skilled carpenter, so he and Blume had been given special permission to leave the Jewish Pale and move to Kiev, where his skills would be available to wealthy urban Russians. Though he had special permission to live in the city, however, the Mabovitses were constrained to live in the city's Jewish ghetto. The Mabovitses fared better than many other Jewish families because Moshe's carpentry skills brought in extra money, but their life was still very hard. Moshe often went unpaid for his work because Jewish workers had no protection under the law. If a client did not pay, there was nothing Moshe could do. Meir recalls how she and her older sister, Shana (known to family members as Sheyna), and her younger sister, Clara (known to family members as Zipke), often went to bed hungry:

> I remember all too clearly how poor we were. There was never enough of anything, not food, not warm clothing, not heat at home. I was always a little too cold outside and a little too empty inside. . . . I can summon up with no effort at all, almost intact, the picture of myself sitting in tears in the kitchen, watching my mother feed some of the gruel that rightfully belonged to me to my younger sister Zipke. Gruel was a great luxury in our home in those days, and I bitterly resented having to share any of it, even with the baby. . . . I am glad that no one told me then that my older sister Sheyna often fainted from hunger in school.[4]

In addition to living with hunger, the family also lived with the fear of the Russian pogroms. The word *pogrom* means devastation in Russian, and during Meir's childhood it usually meant a storm of people sweeping through a town and beating or killing any Jew they could find. Violence against Jews had spread, and there were constant rumors that enraged mobs would sweep through the streets of Kiev. In her autobiography, Meir wrote of how living with the threat of the pogroms instilled in her a belief that survival depended on personal action:

> I must have been very young, maybe only three and a half or four. . . . I can still recall distinctly hearing about a pogrom that was to descend on us. I didn't know then, of course, what a pogrom was, but I knew it had something to do with being Jewish and with the rabble that used to surge through town, brandishing knives and huge sticks, screaming . . . as they looked for the Jews, and who were now going to do terrible things to me and to my family. . . . That pogrom never materialized, but to this day I remember how scared I was and how angry. . . . And,

Jews expelled from a Russian village are forced to relocate to the Jewish Pale. Because of her father's talents as a carpenter, Golda's family did not have to live in the Pale.

Russian Pogroms

The Russian pogroms swept through Jewish communities in a storm of violence and death. This passage, excerpted from Conor Cruise O'Brien's The Siege, *illustrates the chilling fact that the pogroms were sanctioned by the government.*

"In cold figures, and by the standards of our times, the Kishinev pogrom was a nasty, but not outstanding case of licensed brutality: 32 men, 6 women, and 3 children killed outright, 8 persons who later died of wounds, 495 injured, of whom 95 heavily, many (mostly unreported) cases of rape, some mutilation of individual victims, some desecration of sacred objects, much blood and gore, innumerable roving and ecstatic mobs forming and reforming continuously, and vast heaps of debris and filth left over to be cleaned up after the troops had finally moved in and peace had descended on the streets. Damage to property was in due proportion: some 1,500 homes, workshops, and stores looted and destroyed and a large proportion, possibly a fifth of the city's Jewish population, rendered homeless and destitute. . . . [Neither citizens nor officials sought to stop the massacre.] They did not raise a finger to put a stop to the plunder and assaults. They walked calmly along and gazed at [the] horrible spectacle with the utmost indifference. Many of them even rode through the streets in their carriages in holiday attire in order to witness the cruelties that were being perpetrated."

above all, I remember being aware that this was happening to me because I was Jewish. . . . It was a feeling that I was to know again many times during my life—the fear, the frustration, the consciousness of being different and the profound instinctive belief that if one wanted to survive, one had to take effective action about it personally.[5]

As a child, Golda felt powerless, and there seemed to be little her family could do to protect themselves. One of the few actions they could take was to board up their house. As an adult, Golda talked about watching her father nail boards across the windows of their house to protect the family in case the mobs appeared:

I can remember how I stood on the stairs together with a neighbor's daughter of about my own age, holding hands, watching our fathers trying to barricade the entrance by nailing boards across the door. I can hear the sound of that hammer now, and I can

Jewish refugees pass the Statue of Liberty on their way to Ellis Island. Golda's father immigrated to the United States in 1903.

see the children standing in the streets wide-eyed, not making a sound, watching the nails being driven in. . . . I remember how scared I was, and how angry.[6]

The mobs did not come to Golda's house, but they did attack elsewhere. One of the most violent attacks happened in April 1903 in a town called Kishinev. The violence began after rumors circulated that a young woman who had committed suicide had actually been killed by the Jewish family that employed her and that her blood was being used for secret religious ceremonies. These rumors, as untrue as all the others, nevertheless inflamed the barely concealed hostility of the people of Kishinev toward the Jews. They savagely attacked the Jewish citizens of the town. The violence lasted for three days. When it ended, forty-nine Jews were dead, one hundred injured, and two thousand left without homes.

Golda's family listened in horror to the stories of violence and destruction coming

What It Means to Be Jewish

In his personal account of the building of the State of Israel, David Ben-Gurion, first prime minister of Israel, writes of the rich and unique heritage of the Jewish people. The following is excerpted from Ben-Gurion's book Israel: A Personal History.

"In their hearts the Jews retained a feeling of their uniqueness and of their historical mission, though this expressed itself in the religious sphere rather than in terms of modern nationalism. The traditional education that every Jew sought to impart to his sons—though not to his daughters—gave the Jews, consciously or otherwise, a sense of unity and historical continuity, as well as a faith in ultimate salvation. And though Hebrew was not a spoken tongue, it lived in the hearts of the people because it was the language of prayer, poetry, and religious literature, and served as the medium of communication among the Jews of various countries. The religious holidays, rich in national memories, served as a substitute for communal life in the Homeland. There were only a few thousand Jews in the Land of Israel, but every Jew carried the Land of Israel in his soul. Indeed, the land of his fathers was closer to his heart than the land in which he had been born and lived."

David Ben-Gurion served as Israel's first prime minister. The noted statesman was dedicated to establishing a Jewish homeland, as well as to preserving the culture and heritage of the Jewish people.

out of Kishinev. In protest, Jewish communities across the empire held a day-long fast. Five-year-old Golda joined the fast despite her parents' protests that she was too young. The determination to act when events demanded a response stayed with Golda for the rest of her life.

Looking for a Better Life

The Kishinev pogrom convinced Moshe the time to leave Russia had come. Tired of fighting anti-Jewish sentiment and of living with the threat of violence, he decided to take his family to America. There, Moshe felt, they would be free to practice their religion, and he would be free to earn a living. The whole family could not afford to emigrate at the same time, however. So Moshe went first in hopes of finding a job and a home for his family. Once settled, he would send for them. Moshe left in 1903, one of more than 2 million Jews fleeing Russia between 1881 and 1914. By the turn of the century fifty thousand Jews had emigrated from Russia; in 1905 that number jumped to one hundred thousand, and by 1907 it had tripled.

With Moshe's departure, Blume and her daughters moved to the Jewish ghetto in Pinsk, where they lived with Blume's parents. In Pinsk Golda developed much of the revolutionary spirit that would guide her later activities. Golda's sister Shana played an important part in shaping her understanding of right and wrong and the importance of fighting for causes one feels are just. By watching Shana in Pinsk, Golda learned to be a revolutionary and a leader. Pinsk, at the time of the Mabovits family's arrival, was a hotbed of radical ac-

tivity; Pinsk's Jewish writers and educators were demanding change for their people. Fourteen-year-old Shana, swept up in the movement, began attending meetings at the home of the sister of Chaim Weizmann, one of the leaders of the so-called Zionist movement.

Zionists believed that the Jewish should return to their ancient homeland in Palestine and build a nation there. The idea was being promoted around the world by Theodor Herzl, a popular Austrian playwright and journalist and one of the movement's most vocal proponents. In 1897, Herzl wrote an essay for the London *Chronicle* calling for the creation of a Jewish nation:

Theodor Herzl, the founder of modern Zionism. Herzl became convinced that the only solution to European anti-Semitism was to establish an independent Jewish state.

A Home of Their Own

In the following passage excerpted from Conor Cruise O'Brien's The Siege, *Leon Pinsker, a Russian Jew and Zionist, talks of the need for a Jewish homeland.*

"With unbiased eyes and without prejudice we must see in the mirror of the nations the . . . figure of our people . . . with . . . maimed limbs, [who] helps to make universal history without managing properly its own little history. We must reconcile ourselves once and for all to the idea that the other nations, by reason of their inherent . . . antagonism, will forever reject us. We must not shut our eyes to this natural force which works like every other elemental force; we must take it into account. We must not complain of it; on the contrary, we are duty-bound to take courage, to rise and to see to it that we do not remain forever the foundling of the nations."

There are two striking phenomena in our time: high civilization and low barbarism. By high civilization I mean the remarkable achievements of technology that have enabled us to [remain a nation]. By low barbarism I mean anti-Semitism. . . . Everywhere, we Jews have honestly tried to assimilate into nations around us, preserving only the religion of our fathers. We have not been permitted to. . . . We are a nation—the enemy has made us one without our desiring it. . . . We do have the strength to create a state and, moreover, a model state.[7]

After years of living with oppression, the idea of a Jewish state was irresistible to Shana. She began working for the movement, attending secret meetings, delivering leaflets and papers to promote the Zionist cause. Five-year-old Golda watched her sister, and began to pick up her revolutionary ideas:

Sheyna was fourteen when Father left for the states, a remarkable, intense, intelligent girl who became, and who remained, one of the greatest influences of my life—perhaps the greatest. . . . By any standard, she was an unusual person, and for me she was a shining example, my dearest friend and my mentor. . . . At fourteen, Sheyna was a revolutionary, an earnest, dedicated member of the Socialist-Zionist movement, and as such doubly dangerous in the eyes of police and liable to punishment. Not only were she and her friends "conspiring" to overthrow the all-powerful czar, but they also proclaimed their dream to bring into existence a Jewish socialist state in Palestine. In the Russia of the early twentieth century, even a fourteen- or fifteen-year-old schoolgirl who held such views could be arrested for subversive activity, and I still remember

Building a Homeland

Throughout her childhood, Meir dreamed of a Jewish homeland. In an October 1969 speech to workers and union executives at the AFL-CIO convention in Atlantic City, Meir talked of her childhood dream and the price the Jewish people had paid to make their dream a reality. The following is excerpted from Peggy Mann's Golda.

"For two thousand years our people were in exile, always the candidates to be massacred, to be discriminated against, to be second- and third- and tenth-class citizens in all parts of the world. But they had the courage to dream a big dream. One day, we will come back to the land from which we were driven twice before. We will establish there again our sovereignty. We will work with our hands, create everything in that country. We will live at peace with our neighbors and at peace with the entire world."

During her tumultuous childhood in anti-Semitic Russia, Golda Meir longed for a Jewish homeland.

hearing the screams of young men and women being brutally beaten in the police station around the corner from where we lived.[8]

Blume was terrified that Shana's activity would cause the imprisonment and possibly death of the entire family. "Shana was a fabulous person . . . with lots of guts," Clara later wrote about her sister. "She had a tremendous amount of determination. She was a wonderful human being but she was a real danger to our family. She used to distribute revolutionary material. If the [authorities] caught you doing that then it was the end of you and the end of your family."[9]

Blume also worried about Shana's growing attachment to Sam Korngold, one of the local leaders of the movement. In Blume's eyes, Sam was a poor choice for a husband. He had no money and poor prospects for the future. Blume was afraid that if the family stayed in Russia her headstrong daughter would decide to marry the fiery revolutionary.

Going to America

Finally, in 1906, Blume could stand no more. The violence against Jews was increasing and Blume lived in constant fear of both the mobs and of the authorities who might learn about Shana and her revolutionary friends. Blume wrote to Moshe and told him the family must come to America immediately. Moshe was working in Milwaukee as a carpenter, and he had not saved enough money to buy the entire family official exit permits from Russia. But he did have enough to purchase fake permits and buy them passage in an illegal immigration caravan.

Blume knew her family was facing a dangerous trip. Stories had circulated among the Jewish community of the illegal conductors who arranged the trips and then took the immigrants' money and left them stranded in the middle of nowhere. Other stories were even scarier. There were reports of young Jewish girls being kidnapped and sold to brothels in South America and Asia and of immigrants being shot and killed by soldiers as they tried to sneak across the Polish border. Using their fake papers, the family planned to cross the Russian-Polish border at the city of Galicia, then make their way to Vienna and Antwerp, where they would board a ship for Quebec, Canada. If her family could make it across the border into Poland, Blume felt they would be safe.

And so they did, with only one incident. As their train was crossing the border, Russian police searched the passengers looking for fake passports. Blume used most of the money she had saved to bribe the police into letting them across the border. The bribe worked, and the police let Golda's family remain on the train. Once in Poland the family waited for two days in freezing weather in an unheated shack for a train to Antwerp. Finally Blume and her three daughters arrived in Antwerp and boarded their ship. The family had started the last leg of their journey, but their ordeal was not over. Living conditions aboard the ship were terrible. Golda later recalled her first sight of the ship:

> There were sailors dragging and hauling bundles and boxes from the small boat onto the large ship, shouting and thundering as they worked. There were officers giving out orders in loud voices, like trumpets. There were children crying, mothers clutching them, fathers questioning the officers on where they should go. And there seemed to be everything under heaven that had any noise in it come to swell the confusion of sound.[10]

Once onboard, all of the immigrants were ordered below into the ship's dark and crowded interior. Golda's family shared a small cabin with four other people and slept on bunks without sheets. The immigrants spent hours standing in line for what little food was available and everyone was seasick. But despite the hardships, Golda was excited. She was on her way to America.

Chapter

2 A Taste of Freedom

Arriving in America in 1906 was for eight-year-old Golda like walking into a dream. The sidewalks were bustling with people who spoke a strange language and the streets were congested with cars. After the poverty of the Russian ghettos, Milwaukee seemed like a fairy-tale city, full of wealth and activity. The shops were filled with brightly colored ribbons and dresses unlike anything she had seen in her homeland and the grocery stores were brimming with an abundance of foods. In addition to this bewildering array of luxuries, Golda also had to reacquaint herself with the stranger who was her father. In her autobiography, Meir later wrote about her early days in America:

> My father met us in Milwaukee, and he seemed changed: beardless, American-looking, in fact a stranger. . . . Milwaukee—even the small parts of it that I saw during those first few days—overwhelmed me: new food, the baffling sounds of an unfamiliar language, the confusion of getting used to a parent I had almost forgotten. It all gave me a feeling of unreality so strong that I can still remember standing in the street and wondering who and where I was.[11]

There was no time for the family to slowly assimilate to the new culture. Moshe

was proud of how quickly he had adapted to his new homeland. In the three years he had been in America he had found a job as a carpenter for the railroad, joined a synagogue, and become an active member of the community. And he wanted his family to immerse themselves in their new homeland just as quickly. Moshe started working to Americanize his family immediately. The first few days in America set the tone for the family's later relationships, creating tensions and divisions that lasted for years.

Fitting In

Moshe's first step in the transformation was to make his daughters look like Americans. The day after his family arrived, Moshe took his daughters downtown to buy American clothes. He wanted them to give up the black dresses they customarily wore in Russia and dress in the bright colors that were more common in America.

> Refusing to listen to any arguments . . . he determinedly marched all of us downtown on a shopping expedition. He was horrified, he said, by our appearance. We looked so dowdy and "Old World," particularly Sheyna in

A Land of Wonders

Arriving in America was like entering a wonderland. Everywhere Golda looked there were new delights. In her autobiography, Golda talked about her first days in America. The following passage is taken from Golda Meir's My Life.

"Everything looked so colorful and fresh, as though it had just been created, and I stood for hours staring at the traffic and the people. The automobile in which my father had fetched us from the train was the first I had ever ridden in, and I was fascinated by what seemed like the endless procession of cars, trolleys and shiny bicycles on the street. . . . I remember enviously watching a little girl of my own age dressed up in her Sunday best, with puffed sleeves and high-button shoes, proudly wheeling a doll that reclined grandly on a pillow of its own, and marveling at the sight of the women in long white skirts and men in white shirts and neck ties. It was completely strange and unlike anything I had seen or known of before, and I spent the first days in Milwaukee in a kind of a trance."

A Wisconsin avenue bustles with activity in this turn-of-the-century photograph. Golda and her family moved to Milwaukee, Wisconsin, in 1906.

A view of Milwaukee, Wisconsin, at the time Golda and her family lived in the city. The transition from the strict life in Russia to the freedoms in America was overwhelming for the family.

her matronly black dress. He insisted on buying us all new clothes, as though by dressing us differently he could turn us, within twenty-four hours, into three American-looking girls.[12]

For Golda and her sisters, already overwhelmed by their new homeland, the trip was a disaster. Shana already missed Russia and the life she had left behind, and she was not ready to adopt American customs. Seeing the clothes she was expected to wear, Shana burst into tears and shouted, "Maybe that's how you dress in America, but I am certainly not going to dress like that!"[13]

Each member of the family handled the change differently. Five-year-old Clara adapted easily, but for Shana the transition was long and painful. English was difficult for her and learning the language was a struggle. She made few friends in her first years, and she often felt lonely and isolated. She felt like she should have remained in Russia and worked for a Jewish homeland. But for Blume, America offered numerous opportunities. She found the family a house in the Jewish section of the city. The house was small and dark and lacked electricity and a bathroom, but it seemed like a palace compared with their home in Russia. And, most importantly to Blume, the front room of the house was a large empty space that had once been used as a store. Blume saw the empty store as an opportunity and decided to open a neighborhood grocery store. Far from improving their circumstances, Blume's decision only added to the tensions within the family.

Moshe took his wife's idea as a personal insult. He believed Blume wanted to open the store because she did not think he could support her and the children. Moshe refused to help in any way with the store. Blume's decision also caused another round of battles between Shana and her mother. Shana thought that merchants were only interested in making money at the expense of poor workers who could not afford to pay the high prices. To her, Blume's store represented everything she hated about Russia. "I did not come to America to turn into a shopkeeper, a social parasite,"[14] Shana told her parents. Instead of helping with the store or going to school, Shana decided to follow her socialist beliefs and take a job in a factory, where she could work among laborers.

For Golda, the move to America roused many conflicting feelings. She was torn between her loyalty and love for her sister, her love for her parents, and the excitement she felt about the new world opening up around her.

Freedoms and Obligations

The tension in the family increased when Blume refused to heed her family's disapproval. Blume was determined to open the store even without her family's support. Without telling Moshe, she borrowed money from a local moneylender and opened the grocery store. The store was an instant success and the extra money helped support the family whenever Moshe was between jobs. But the hours were long and the work was hard; every morning Blume had to leave home before dawn to buy fruits and vegetables from local wholesale markets. These trips often kept her away from home until late in the

morning and someone had to open the store and tend it until she returned. Since both Moshe and Shana refused to have anything to do with the store, the job fell to eight-year-old Golda.

Golda hated working at the store. It made her late for school, and to Golda school was the most wonderful thing about America. In Russia, Golda had not attended school, and it opened a new world for her. "Golda loved school," her sister Clara told Golda's biographers. "She was conscientious and good in every subject." As an adult, Meir explained the magic she found in school: "I found freedom, kindness and cleanliness. . . . It was [at school] I first experienced a lack of prejudice. . . . In America, I lost my terror of Pinsk and Kiev."[15]

In her autobiography, Meir wrote about what she learned in those early years at her first American school.

> It isn't really important to decide when you are very young just exactly what you want to become when you grow up. . . . It is much more important to decide on the way you want to live. If you are going to be honest with yourself and honest with your friends, if you are going to get involved with causes which are good for others, not only for yourselves, then it seems to me that is sufficient, and maybe what you will be is only a matter of chance.[16]

Golda tried to explain to her mother that students were not allowed to be late for class, but Blume would not listen. Not even calls from school officials could change her mind. In Blume's opinion, education was not important for girls and Golda's first duty was to her family. To Blume, the few hours Golda spent in the store were much more important than the time she spent in the classroom. Golda resented being forced to work in the store and miss class, and tension between her and her mother grew.

Strained Relationships

The stress of the first four years in Milwaukee split the family apart. Shana refused to fit into the life the family was building, and her parents were unable to understand her feelings. While Golda and Clara enjoyed sledding parties with their friends or an occasional movie at the local theater, Shana worked and saved her money for the day when she could leave. The tension peaked when Shana found a letter her mother had written to an American relative of a friend in Pinsk saying she hoped he and Shana might marry. Furious at her mother's matchmaking, Shana tore up the letter and decided to leave home. She soon moved to Chicago, where she found a job in a men's clothing factory as a seamstress. But when an infected cut on her hand left her sick and unable to work, she had to return home. Clara later defended her parents:

> They had a problem with . . . kids who weren't easy to raise. My father was a wonderful person but he was never a breadwinner. My mother knew what it was not to have money and she wanted her daughters to have an easier life. She wasn't looking for anything for herself; she was trying to find a way to make it easier for them. Maybe she didn't use the best judgement. Maybe she didn't size up the daughters she had to do business with. But she was a typical Jewish mother, and worried about them.[17]

While Shana was away, Golda intensely missed her sister. When Shana returned, Golda helped care for her and the two became even closer. Golda still idolized Shana and listened tirelessly to her dreams about a homeland for the Jewish people and her commitment to the socialist ideals of a society where everyone worked for the good of the community and where everyone's basic needs of clothing and shelter were met. Shana also shared her feelings for Sam Korngold, the young rebel leader she had left behind in Russia. Shana had continued to write to him in secret, despite her

A young Golda Meir poses for a somber photograph. Golda grew to womanhood while living in the United States.

mother's disapproval of him. While recuperating at home, Shana received a letter from one of her aunts in Pinsk, telling her that Sam had been arrested by the Russian authorities, had escaped, and was heading for New York. Along with the letter, her aunt enclosed Sam's New York address. Shana was elated. She wrote to Sam and invited him to move to Milwaukee.

When Blume found out, she was furious. But Shana was as determined as her mother. Once again, Shana found a job and left her parents' home. As soon as she could, she rented a room for Sam, and as soon as he arrived in Milwaukee, she enrolled both of them in night English classes.

For a short time it looked as if everyone in Golda's family might be happy. But then Shana became sick again, and this time her illness was serious. She had tuberculosis. Some 154,000 people were dying of the bacterial disease each year, and more than a million people were infected. There was at the time no cure, and the only treatment was fresh air, nutritious food, and lots of rest. Golda was terrified her sister would die, with good reason: 25 percent of tuberculosis patients died and only 50 percent of those who lived were completely cured.

The National Jewish Hospital for Consumptives, or people with tuberculosis, had opened in Denver to treat patients who could not afford hospital care elsewhere. Blume and Moshe decided that the hospital was the only hope for their sick daughter, so they sent Shana to Denver. Shana went to the hospital filled with fear; she left Milwaukee wondering if she would ever see her family or Sam again. She also left Wisconsin without healing the rift with her parents. While Shana was in the hospital, she never spoke to her parents, and the only contact she had with her family was through letters that she secretly exchanged with Golda. The two sisters were able to keep in contact with the middleman help of one of Golda's school friends, Regina.

Fighting for an Education

Golda wrote Shana long letters filled with stories about her life at school and a little news about home. Even in America, the land of opportunity, the family was struggling. Moshe often had trouble finding work and earning money. Golda often hoarded her school money to buy stamps to mail letters to Shana. While money was tight and life hard, Golda realized that there were children even poorer than she who could not afford school books. Although school was free in the early 1900s, students were expected to buy their own textbooks.

Inspired by Shana's political views and her activities in Russia, eleven-year-old Golda decided to help the students who had no money for books. She organized a group of her school friends to raise money. Golda called the group the American Young Sister's Society because she thought the name sounded impressive and would make people listen to her. Golda and her friend Regina made hand-lettered signs announcing an evening of entertainment to raise money to buy textbooks for the needy. "Nothing in life happens," she later said. "It isn't enough to believe in something. You have to have the stamina to meet obstacles and overcome them. . . . What you do is what you are." [18]

Though she was only a child, Golda was already a persuasive organizer. She convinced the owner of a local meeting hall to donate its use for one night for her fund-raiser. The hall was packed that night. Some people came because their children had helped organize it, some because it was free entertainment, and many out of curiosity to see what kind of event a group of children had organized. Participants did what they could; some recited poetry, others recited bits of plays from memory, and some sang. Even six-year-old Clara recited a poem. The highlight of the night was when Golda mounted the stage and made an impassioned plea for money to buy textbooks and spoke of the need for education for everyone.

The event was a success and made the front page of the local newspaper, which reported, "A score of little children gave their playtime and scant pennies to charity, a charity organized by their own initiative too. . . . And it is worthy of comment that this charity is itself a loud comment on the fact that little children may go to public schools without proper possession of books. Think what that means." [19]

Golda the leader, Golda the organizer, Golda the impassioned speaker made her debut that night. She wrote to Shana that the fund-raiser was "the greatest success . . . and the entertainment was grand." [20]

Runaway

Education remained one of Golda's primary goals for the next few years. No matter how many hours she worked at the store or other jobs, she continued to excel at school. Her hard work paid off and Golda was named valedictorian at her eighth-grade graduation. This was a major triumph for Golda, and she was looking forward to high school. But her success was causing more problems at home and it was becoming a battle for her to continue her education. "My mother didn't want me to have an education," Meir later said. "She thought it was for men only. [Women were supposed to] marry, marry, marry, while quite young." [21] Golda was the first person in her family to graduate from elementary school. It was a great achievement, and to her parents it was the end of her education. But to Golda it was just a beginning.

Golda dreamed of going to high school and then becoming a teacher. Her parents wanted her to go to secretarial school and become a secretary until she could be married. Golda fought, argued, cried, and eventually enrolled at North Division High School in the fall of 1912 without her parents' permission. She worked afternoons and weekends at a variety of jobs and taught English to immigrants for ten cents an hour to pay for her high school books and supplies. Blume thought her daughter was a foolish rebel who should settle into the traditional roles of wife and mother. While Golda was attending high school, Blume became determined to find her a husband. The most likely prospect was a Mr. Goodstein, a man in his early thirties who was relatively prosperous, someone Blume felt would be able to care for her daughter. Fourteen-year-old Golda indignantly refused to consider marrying a man who was more than twice

her age. Angry at her rebellious daughter, Blume insisted Golda quit school.

In despair Golda wrote to her sister. Shana's health had improved enough for her to leave the hospital and marry Sam. The couple were now living in Denver near the hospital. Golda's brother-in-law wrote to her, "You shouldn't stop school. You are too young to work; you have good chances to become something. . . . You should get ready to come to us. We are not rich either, but you will have good chances here to study and we will do all we can for you." [22]

Golda was convinced, but she knew it was useless to ask her parents' permission. They still thought of Sam as a starry-eyed revolutionary and of Shana as a rebellious daughter. There was no way they would let Golda move to Denver or continue her education. In desperation, Golda decided to run away from home. Staying at home would mean the end of her education, and Golda intended to follow her dreams. So she made her plans carefully, following Shana's advice that

Golda Meir (second from left) as a young student-teacher in Milwaukee, Wisconsin. As a child, Golda dreamed of becoming a teacher.

"the main thing is never to be excited. Always be calm and act coolly. The way of action will always bring you good results. Be brave."[23] Golda would follow that advice throughout her life.

Sam and Shana sent Golda part of the money needed for a train ticket and Golda raised the rest by borrowing money from a friend and giving more English lessons. When she had enough money for the ticket, she put her plans in motion. Golda "lowered her small suitcase out of [her window] at ten o'clock at night," Regina told one of Golda's biographers. "I took it home and hid it in the bushes. Then, in the morning, she called on me to go to school as always, but we picked up her suitcase and took the trolley to Union Station. Years later, I sent her a picture of Union Station, just to remind her."[24]

3 Educating a Rebel

Denver promised everything that the fourteen-year-old Golda yearned for. There she was given a chance to study, to learn and expand her view of the world, and there Golda's political awareness fully developed. "Denver was a turning point because my real education began there," she later said. "In Denver, life really opened up for me." [25]

In Sam and Shana's home Golda was immersed in politics, philosophy, and religious history. She was exposed to a group of people who believed that everyone had the ability and the duty to change the world for the better. Golda would stay up late at night listening to her sister's friends debate the state of the world and how it ought to be.

A Growing Awareness

In her autobiography, Meir described her sister's house:

Sheyna's small apartment had become a kind of center in Denver for the Jewish immigrants from Russia who had come out west for treatment. . . . Some of them were anarchists, some were socialists, and some were Socialist Zion-

ists. . . . They all had either been ill or were still ill; they all were uprooted, they all were passionately and vitally concerned with the major issues of the day. They talked, argued and even quarreled for hours about what was happening in the world and what ought to happen. [26]

In all the heady political discussion, it was Zionist ideas that held Golda's attention. Shana's friends talked of building a homeland for the Jewish people, a place where Jews could be free and independent. They talked of pioneers who had already moved to Palestine to build a Jewish homeland. The idea of a small group of men and women trying to carve a new home out of the desert sparked Golda's imagination. She began spending more and more time with Shana's friends and began dating some of the young men who regularly visited the house. Many of the younger men in the group became infatuated with her. They took her to lectures, to concerts, and for long walks in the park. Some of them even proposed to her, but Golda was more interested in political causes than romantic relationships, and she treated most of her suitors simply as friends. Golda's feelings changed, however, when she met twenty-one-year-old

Golda and her future husband, Morris Meyerson. Golda admired Meyerson's maturity and his knowledge of the arts and literature.

Morris Meyerson, a soft-spoken and dreamy young man who came often to Shana and Sam's.

Golda and Morris were temperamental and intellectual opposites. Golda was stormy and determined, Morris was calm and philosophical. Golda was interested in politics and current events, Morris was interested in classical music and poetry. But the two were drawn to each other immediately. Morris was attracted to Golda's outspoken and fiery spirit, Golda to Morris's quiet intelligence and maturity. He spent long hours with Golda discussing literature, history, and philosophy. He introduced her to classical music, and during the summer of 1914 they spent Sunday afternoons together listening to free concerts in the parks around Denver. Morris introduced her to music, the arts, and literature, and the sixteen-year-old Golda fell in love:

I admired Morris enormously—more than I had ever admired anyone except Sheyna—not only for his encyclopedic knowledge, but for his gentleness, his intelligence and his wonderful sense of humor. He was only five or six years my senior, but he seemed much older, much calmer and much steadier. Without at first being aware of what was happening to me, I fell in love with him and couldn't help realizing that he loved me, too, although for a long time we said nothing to each other about the way we felt.[27]

The hours Golda spent listening to political debates at Shana's or attending concerts with Morris seemed a world away from the hours she spent during the day attending school. Golda's school, North Side High School, was made up mostly of wealthy non-Jewish students who did not share her interests in education and the Zionist cause. Golda, for her part, had no interest in football, social hours, and dances. The constant shifting between these two worlds troubled Golda but she did not allow it to interfere with her education. She excelled in her classes, earning A's in English, algebra, Latin, ancient history, music, and German in her first semester. But slowly Golda's long nights listening to the philosophers in Shana's kitchen and the hours she spent with Morris stole time from her schoolwork. Golda did not mind, because she felt she was learning more from the people she was meeting than she could learn in school. But Shana, who saw herself as Golda's guardian and surrogate mother, did mind. Shana frequently lectured and badgered Golda about attending school, doing her homework, getting plenty of sleep, and staying out late with young men. Even though Shana had been a rebel most of her life, she believed deeply in some of the conservative attitudes of her parents. She saw it as her duty to mother Golda and see that she behaved properly. The two sisters began to argue frequently. Both shared some of their mother's stubbornness and unwillingness to compromise. The quarrels became more frequent and more heated.

On Her Own

"Shana thought that what she said was direct from God," Golda's friend Regina later told one of Golda's biographers. "She was always driving people to do things according to her precise standards, constantly criticizing. She could be a very hard person, dogmatic and domineering, often very difficult and very selfish like her mother. She was not a warm person. I know somebody who once called her a lemon."[28] The arguments escalated during the year Golda lived with her sister until, at the age of sixteen, Golda decided it was time to live on her own.

One day, after [Shana] had been particularly bossy, ordering me about and scolding me as though I were still a child, I decided that the time had come for me to try to live alone, without a mother hen and without being nagged all the time, and I marched out of the apartment in the black skirt and white blouse I had been wearing all day without taking anything else with me, not even a nightgown. If I was leaving . . . [Shana's] home and authority, I was not entitled, I thought, to keep anything that [Shana and Sam] had bought for me. I closed the door behind me, and that, I thought, was that:

I was on my own at last. It was something of a comedown to realize ten minutes later that now I had to find somewhere to live until I could support myself. A little crestfallen but very grateful, I accepted the invitation extended by two of [Shana's] friends who had always been especially nice to me and to whom I confided that for the moment I was homeless.[29]

Life on her own was harder than Golda anticipated. She had left Milwaukee so that she could attend school, but total independence in Denver meant giving up her dream of education. For Golda the choice was either to find a job or to return to her sister's home. Too stubborn and too proud to beg her sister's forgiveness, Golda quit school and took a full-time job at a local laundry. The work was hard, the clothes were washed by hand on scrub boards, and many nights she came home with bleeding hands, but it paid six dollars a week. With her first week's wages Golda was able to move into a small rented room on her own. Finally, with Morris's prompting, Golda found a job in a Denver department store where she sold dresses and took measurements for alterations. Though she worked nine hours a day, the job was less physically demanding than laundry work.

Despite the long hours Golda found time to immerse herself in political causes. Reports were reaching Denver that more Jewish settlers were headed for the Holy Land of Palestine. They were moving into

The Dream Is Alive

A mass meeting to celebrate the impending passage of the Balfour Declaration was held at the London Opera House. Lord Cecil, a British official, attended the meeting and discussed his feelings about the declaration. The following is excerpted from Ronald Sanders's The High Walls of Jerusalem.

"[This is] the first constructive effort that we have made in what I hope will be the new settlement of the world after the war. I do not say that is the only thing involved. It is not only the recognition of a nationality, it is much more than that. It has great underlying ideals of which you will hear this afternoon, and of which it would be impertinent of me to speak. It is, indeed, not the birth of a nation, for the Jewish nation through centuries of oppression and captivity have preserved their sentiment of nationality as few peoples could: but if it is not the birth of a nation, I believe we may say it is the re-birth of a nation. I don't like to prophesy what ultimate results that great event may have, but for myself I believe it will have a far-reaching influence on the history of the world and consequences which none can foresee on the future history of the human race."

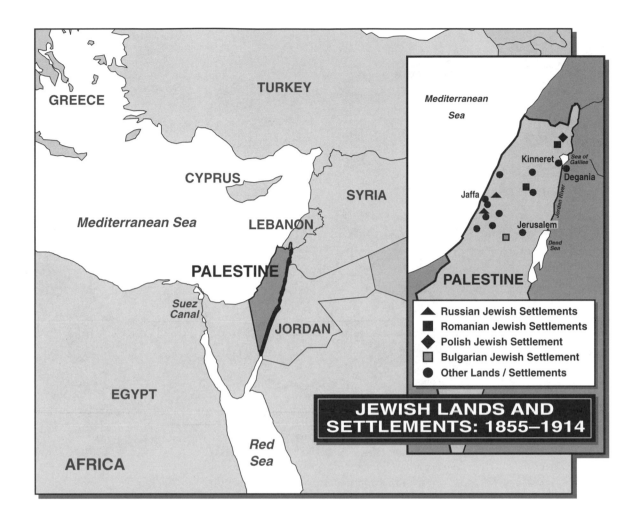

JEWISH LANDS AND SETTLEMENTS: 1855–1914

Map labels: GREECE, TURKEY, CYPRUS, SYRIA, Mediterranean Sea, LEBANON, PALESTINE, Suez Canal, JORDAN, EGYPT, Red Sea, AFRICA

Inset map labels: Mediterranean Sea, Kinneret, Sea of Galilee, Degania, Jaffa, Jordan River, Jerusalem, Dead Sea, PALESTINE

Legend:
▲ Russian Jewish Settlements
■ Romanian Jewish Settlements
◆ Polish Jewish Settlement
▨ Bulgarian Jewish Settlement
● Other Lands / Settlements

the area illegally, for Palestine had been ruled by the Ottoman Turks since the sixteenth century, and the Turkish government did not welcome Jewish settlers. But though the Turkish government opposed the Jewish migration, still the settlers came. The migration had started in the 1880s; by 1914 over 115,000 Jews had moved into the area. Jews around the world were sending money to help the immigrants. Golda spent hours standing on street corners with a small blue-and-white box marked Jewish National Fund, collecting donations to send to the settlers in

Palestine. The Jewish National Fund's purpose was to raise money to buy land in Palestine for the settlers. Most of the land the fund was able to purchase appeared worthless. The land was either too rocky to grow crops on or was part of eroded hillsides or malarial marshes. But worthless acreage was the only land the Turkish and Arab landowners would sell to the settlers. And even this useless land was sold at exorbitant prices. But still the settlers traveled to Palestine determined to carve a home out of the worthless soil. And Golda listened to the stories of their efforts with

This early–nineteenth-century photograph shows Arab men, women, and children collecting rocks to build a road in Palestine. Most Arabs resented the Jewish immigrants and would sell them only worthless lands.

growing excitement. It seemed at last as if the Jewish people might actually be able to build their own homeland.

Homesick

Golda's excitement over her new freedom and her dedication to the Zionist cause were tempered by her growing loneliness. She missed Shana and Sam and she missed her family. She had begun corresponding with her mother, but her father refused to write and Blume informed Golda that he would not allow her name to be mentioned in the house. Then one day, about a year after Golda had left Shana's, a surprising letter came from Golda's father. Golda had been careful not to tell her parents that she had quit school and that she was working in a department store, but somehow they had found out. Golda's parents were worried about their stubborn daughter, and the worry and stress were beginning to make Blume ill. Later Golda recounted her response to Moshe's letter informing her that if she valued her mother's life she would return home:

> I understood that for him to write to me at all meant swallowing his pride and he would only have done so if I were really needed at home. So Morris and I talked it over, and I decided that I should go back—to Milwaukee, to my parents and Clara and to high school. To be quite frank, I was not sorry to return, although it meant leaving Morris, who had to stay on in Denver for a while till his sister recovered. One night before I left, Morris told me shyly that he was in love with me and wanted to marry me. I explained happily and just as shyly that I loved him, too, but that I was still much too young for marriage, and we agreed that we would have to wait. In the meantime, we would keep our relationship a secret and write to each other all the time. So I left for Milwaukee in what I told Regina the next day was a blissful state of mind.[30]

Back Home Again

Golda returned to Milwaukee in 1914 to a changed family. Her parents were willing to let her return to school and acknowledged that she was old enough to decide how she wanted to live her life. If Golda wanted to be a teacher, they would not try to stop her. Her family also was doing better financially; they had moved into a newer and larger apartment, and some of the money worries had eased. Nevertheless, many problems still remained and there was still friction between Golda and her mother. Blume felt it was her right to know everything about Golda's life, including her relationship with Morris. When Golda refused to tell her anything, Blume made Clara translate Morris's letters from English into Yiddish (the language commonly spoken by central and eastern European Jews) and read them to her. From that point on, Golda had Morris send all his letters to Regina's house. And Golda never forgave her mother for invading her privacy.

During this time Golda also got involved with the socialist and Zionist political group Poale Zion. Members of the Poale Zion believed that Jews needed their own homeland and committed themselves to making that homeland a reality in Palestine. Golda struggled with her own conscience before joining the group. She believed that before becoming a member of the Poale Zion she had to commit herself to immigrating to Palestine, and at first she was not ready to make the commitment. Unready to join, she began attending meetings and doing volunteer work with the group. Golda taught at the group's Folkshule, a school dedicated to teaching Jewish children about their heritage. Through her work with the school, Golda became more dedicated to the Poale Zion's vision. Finally, a few months before Golda turned eighteen, she was ready to become a full member of the Poale Zion and commit to immigrating to Palestine.

Morris was not happy when he heard the news. He did not believe it was possible for Jews to build their own homeland. In August 1915 he wrote to his future wife, "I do not know whether to say that I am glad or sorry that you have joined the Zionist Party. . . . I am altogether passive

In an August 1915 letter, taken from Ralph G. Martin's Golda Meir, *Morris describes his feelings about Golda joining the Poale Zion, a political group dedicated to the ideals of Zionism.*

"I do not know whether to say that I am glad or sorry that you have joined the Zionist Party, and that you seem to be so enthusiastic a nationalist. I am altogether passive in the matter, though I give you full credit for your activity, as I do to all others engaged in doing something toward helping a distressed nation. . . . The idea of Palestine or any other territory for the Jews is, to me, ridiculous. . . . The other day I received a notice to attend one of the meetings . . . but since I do not care particularly as to whether the Jews are going to suffer in Russia or the Holy Land, I did not go."

in the matter. . . . The idea of Palestine or any other territory for the Jews is, to me, ridiculous."[31] Golda was unswayed by Morris's letter. She was certain that in time Morris would become as committed to the Zionist cause as she. She continued to work tirelessly for the group. She also continued to excel in high school and upon graduation in 1916 she enrolled in the Milwaukee Normal School for training as a teacher.

World War I

Golda's life in Milwaukee was peaceful, but the wider world was preparing for war. What began as a local conflict between the European countries of Austria-Hungary and Serbia in the summer of 1914 quickly spread into a global conflict. Fulfilling alliances made in the aftermath of an earlier war, the world's great and small powers chose up sides in what became World War I. Almost no part of the world was untouched by the war. In all, twenty-seven countries on five continents participated. Fighting took place from Russia to France and even reached into Palestine.

As news of the war circulated, horror stories about Jewish victims of the war also began trickling back to America from Europe. The pogroms that Golda had feared so much in her childhood were escalating and European Jews were victims of both sides of the war. The Jewish Pale of Settlement, where Golda's family had lived, lay in the territory where fighting was heaviest between the Russian and German-Austrian armies. When the Russian army retreated, its soldiers killed Jews in the section suspected of being German sympathizers. When the Russians swept back through the area, the Germans fled and killed Jews suspected of being Russian spies.

Golda's family joined other American Jews in raising money to help the Jews of

Europe. Golda and her father began working with the Jewish Relief Society to raise money for food and clothes for the victims in Europe by going door to door asking for donations. Blume baked homemade food and made mementos for young Jewish soldiers going off to join the war. According to Golda's autobiography:

> During World War I my mother turned our house into a makeshift depot for the boys who had volunteered for the Jewish Legion and were going to fight under the Jewish flag within the framework of the British army to liberate Palestine from the Turks. Most of the young men from Milwaukee who joined the legion [a group of immigrants who were exempt from the draft] left our house equipped with little bags embroidered by my mother in which they kept their prayer shawls . . .

Soldiers defend their positions during World War I. Golda's family became heavily involved in helping both Jewish soldiers and European civilians during the war.

and much larger bags full of cookies still warm from her oven. With an open heart, she ran an open house, and when I try to remember her at this period, I hear the sound of her laughter in the kitchen as she fried onions, peeled carrots and chopped fish for Friday night, talking to one of the guests who would be sleeping on our living-room couch for the weekend.[32]

Through their work with the Jewish Relief Society and their daughter's endless talk about the Zionist cause, Blume and Moshe also became more involved in the Zionist movement. Jewish speakers from around the world who came to speak to the large Jewish community in Milwaukee were invited to stay at their house. Golda listened to every speaker with rapt attention, and she was soon caught up in a whirl of political activism.

Leadership and Activism

Golda's political leadership reached a peak in 1917 when news reached Wiscon-

Jews lie dead after a pogrom in Russia in 1919. News of such pogroms prompted Golda to organize a protest march, which gained momentum among both Jews and Christians.

The Work Has Just Begun

In a newspaper article published in January 1918, Zionist leader David Ben-Gurion rejoices at the Balfour Declaration, but cautions the Jewish people that the declaration is only the first step toward the birth of a Jewish nation. The newspaper article is excerpted from Ben-Gurion's Israel: A Personal History.

"From a political viewpoint, we have been granted our national desire. The declaration issued by the English will soon be ratified by other peoples. We are still confronted by crucial challenges, but not in that sphere. The Zionist task vis-a-vis the outside world has, in a very basic sense, been completed. The question of the link between the people of Israel and the Land of Israel, and the question of revitalizing the ancient Jewish Homeland, has been placed on the world's agenda and will never be removed until the problem is solved to the benefit of the Jewish people, as historical justice demands.

Zionism now has a second task, which is *more important, more serious, and more difficult:* putting Zionist realization on the agenda of every individual Jew: *connecting the creation of a Homeland with the fate of the Jewish masses.*

Zionism must now look inward, focusing on the Jewish people. Every material and spiritual resource must now be devoted to the urgent and demanding task of *building* a Homeland."

sin that a new wave of pogroms was taking place in Poland and Ukraine. One of the worst incidents happened near Golda's old home in Pinsk. Forty Jews were lined up near the wall of a church and shot. The church was in the neighborhood where she once lived, and Golda later learned that some of those killed had been friends and neighbors of her family. "I remember my grandfather's house . . . facing the church. So whenever I think of it, I think of these men,"[33] she said.

In response, Golda organized a protest march. Such demonstrations were rare in this period. Her father begged her not to go through with her plans, fearing that she would embarrass herself and the entire Jewish community. Golda felt that her protest would catch the attention and win the sympathy of the entire city, and it did. The day of the march both Jews and Christians joined together to protest the execution in Pinsk. Hundreds of people representing more than fifty organizations joined the march, which gained national publicity.

It turned out to be an extremely successful parade. It came as a surprise to me . . . that so many non-Jews participated in that [parade] and I can remember looking into the eyes of the people who lined the street watching us and feeling how supportive they were. There weren't many protest marches in those days, and we got publicity all over America.[34]

The news from Europe, coupled with her work with the Poale Zion, crystallized Golda's resolve. The World Zionist Organization was calling for a third wave of immigrants to move to Palestine. Golda decided the time to act had arrived. She quit school and announced her decision to immigrate to Palestine and join one of the small agricultural cooperatives called kibbutzim. "I think it was while we were marching through town that day that I realized I could no longer postpone a final decision about Palestine," she later wrote.

> However hard it might be for those who were dearest to me, I could no longer put off making up my mind about where I was going to live. Palestine, I felt, not parades in Milwaukee, was the only real, meaningful answer. . . . The Jews must have a land of their own again—and I must help build it, not by making speeches or raising funds, but by living and working there.[35]

Making the decision was easy compared with the work needed to get her there. Before she could emigrate, Golda needed to raise the money for her trip, and while the war was going on it would be impossible to travel to Palestine. But more than money and politics stood between Golda and her dream. Golda was set on moving to Palestine, and Morris was equally set on not going. The couple argued, each trying to persuade the other to change, but neither would concede. The arguments ended temporarily when Ben Shapiro, one of the leaders of the Zionist movement in Chicago, asked Golda to come to Chicago to advance the Zionist cause.

Working Toward Her Goal

Golda left Morris, who had moved to Milwaukee to be with her, and moved in with Shapiro's family in Chicago. She worked afternoons as an assistant librarian at the Chicago Public Library to raise money for her trip to Palestine. As soon as her workday ended at the library, she threw herself into Zionist activities. The schedule she kept in Chicago was grueling. Sometimes Poale Zion meetings would last until 4 A.M.; then Golda would rush home to get a few hours sleep before returning to the library. As involved as she was, Golda still missed Morris. And he missed her too. After a few months Morris moved to Chicago to be with Golda again. And once again they argued over Palestine. Morris insisted that Golda's dream of building a Jewish state was a fantasy, and he would not move to Palestine for a fantasy. But on November 2, 1917, the fantasy seemed closer than ever to becoming a reality with the British announcement of the Balfour Declaration.

4 To Palestine

The Balfour Declaration marked the first time any country had officially supported the idea of a homeland for the Jewish people in Palestine. When Great Britain issued the document in November 1917, the Zionist cause for the first time gained legitimacy in the international political arena. For Meir and thousands of other Jews, the declaration seemed to be the culmination of all their hopes.

A few days after the declaration was issued, a young Jewish leader named David Ben-Gurion, the man who would become Israel's first prime minister, wrote an article for *Der Yiddische Kempfer*, an American Zionist newspaper. Ben-Gurion's article summarized the importance of the declaration:

> England has done a great deal: she has recognized our existence as a political entity and our right to the country. *The Jewish people must now transform this recognition into a living reality*, by investing their strength, spirit, energy, and capital in building a National Home and achieving full national salvation.[36]

A British Declaration

Britain had several reasons for supporting the formation of a Jewish homeland in

Arthur Balfour, foreign secretary for Great Britain and author of the Balfour Declaration. The declaration announced Great Britain's support for a Jewish homeland in Palestine.

Palestine. Officially, the Balfour Declaration was issued to thank Dr. Chaim Weizmann, a leader of the Zionist movement and a chemist, for his scientific research on Britain's behalf during World War I. The British government also had a practical reason for its support: A Jewish state created with British assistance would assure Britain a strong presence in a strategically important region.

British soldiers relax in the Jewish section of Palestine in 1929. These soldiers protected Jewish immigrants from the Arab nationals who protested their presence.

The Balfour Declaration, written by Lord Arthur Balfour, the British foreign secretary, stated: "His Majesty's Government view[s] will favour the establishment in Palestine of a national home for the Jewish people, and will use their best endeavors to facilitate the achievement of this object."[37]

Britain acted quickly on its declaration. On December 9, 1917, British forces marched into Jerusalem and took possession of the city from Turkish forces. By the summer of 1918, all of Palestine came un-

der British military rule. With British support for a Jewish homeland in Palestine, and Palestine under British control, Zionists around the world rejoiced. Finally, it seemed, a Jewish state would actually be established.

But their joy was tempered with the knowledge of the long struggle ahead. The land claimed by the Jews was surrounded by Muslim states, and in some cases still held by Muslim landowners, all of whom rejected any Jewish presence in the area. The Jewish people knew that it would take

Pioneering Spirit

In Israel: A
Personal History,
*David Ben-Gurion
talks of the spirit and
determination of the
early immigrants.*

"The men of the First Aliya [wave of Israeli immigrants to
Palestine] . . . differed widely in education, in values, and
in cultural background from most of the men in the Second Aliya. . . . But deep down in their hearts, they were
one and the same; the selfsame revolutionaries and men
of action. Men whom no reality can subjugate, no diffi-
culty daunt. Their spirit is alive and responsive to great
ideas and the challenge of the future."

*Volunteers build fences for a new settlement in 1937. The Jews
who immigrated to Palestine, many of whom had experienced
persecution in Europe, were highly motivated to build a successful
homeland.*

Harsh Realities

Golda's first view of Palestine came at the end of a long and difficult journey from America. She described her first glimpse of the Jewish homeland in My Life.

"There we were—after that terrible journey—in Tel Aviv at last. Our dreams had come true. The railway station, the houses we could see in the distance, even the deep sand that surrounded us all were part of the Jewish national home. But as we waited there in the glaring sun, not knowing where to go or even where to turn, it was hard to remember just why we had come. Someone in our group . . . turned to me and said, only half-jokingly, 'Well Goldie, you wanted to come to [Palestine]. . . . Here we are. Now we can all go back—it's enough.' "

more than words to build a homeland. As Ben-Gurion had written in 1917, it was going to take hard work and dedicated people to build a homeland.

Working for Zion

Meir had the energy, the strength, and the spirit that Ben-Gurion wrote about, and she was ready to dedicate her life to making the dream of Israel a reality. She also agreed, finally, to devote herself to Morris, who could no longer call Meir's dreams a fantasy. He knew he must commit to Palestine or lose Meir. Morris agreed to go to Palestine and the couple was married on December 24, 1917, at Meir's parents' house in Milwaukee. Meir was so committed to the Zionist cause that she rewrote her wedding vows to include the promise that she and Morris would both immigrate to Palestine. Meir adopted the surname Meyerson and began her political life in Is-

rael. Years later, she would change Meyerson to the Hebrew name Meir.

While Golda possessed the desire and energy, she and Morris still lacked the money necessary to travel from the United States to Palestine. Meir was torn between her desire to work for the Zionist cause and her need to find a job to raise money for her trip. The ideal solution came when the Poale Zion offered her a full-time job traveling across the United States and organizing new branches of the group. The job paid fifteen dollars a week plus expenses. These were low wages, but Meir leaped at the opportunity. Even though the job meant being separated from her new husband, Meir knew the money would help pay for their trip to Palestine. And, while she worked to save money, Meir also would be working for the Zionist cause. But what seemed like an ideal solution to Meir seemed outrageous to her family. Her trips for the Poale Zion took her away from Milwaukee, and Morris, for months at a time. Blume and Moshe thought it was disgraceful for a young woman to travel around the country alone. Even Shana, who had once been the most outspoken of revolutionaries, disapproved. Shana wrote to Golda warning her sister to spend less time on political causes and more time with her family. In one letter Shana wrote: "As far as personal happiness is concerned, grasp it, Goldie, and hold it tight. . . . The only thing I heartily wish you is that you should not try to be what you *ought* to be but what you are."[38] But Golda was committed to the cause and Morris was willing to remain in Milwaukee while she worked for the Zionist movement.

Meir later acknowledged that her travels were difficult for her new husband, who cared little for politics and only wanted a quiet life, but she was exhilarated with her work:

> For Morris my frequent absences must have been very difficult, but he was immensely patient and understanding. . . . Whenever I was out of town, I wrote long letters to him, but they tended to be more about the meeting I had just addressed or the one I was about to address, the situation in Palestine or the movement than about us or our relationship. Morris consoled himself for my being away so much by turning our tiny apartment into the real home that awaited me whenever I was in Milwaukee.[39]

Meir traveled by train across the United States and into Canada, spreading Poale Zion's twin messages of Zionism and socialism. In the towns she visited, she slept in the homes of organization members because Poale Zion could not afford to pay for hotels. She gave speeches on the Zionist movement, organized branches of the Poale Zion, recruited new members, and raised money to start a national Jewish newspaper, *Die Zeit* (*The Times*). Even when she was in Milwaukee, Meir kept herself busy with organization business. She attended organization meetings four to five times a week, and on weekends frequently had informal parties at her house for Poale members. Meir was so active, and so dedicated to the Zionist cause, that the organization appointed her one of its delegates to the first meeting of the American Jewish Congress (AJC) in 1918 held to help Jews in Europe. In later years, Meir described her work with the Poale Zion and her part in the World Jewish Congress (an international organization that includes the AJC) as some of the happiest times in her life. She was one of the most popular speakers at the conference, and her speeches moved many of the audience members to tears. Meir wrote to Morris that "some moments [at the convention] reached such heights that after them one could have died happy."[40]

One Step Closer to Zion

Golda continued her work with the Poale Zion until 1920, when she, Morris, her childhood friend Regina, and Regina's fiancé Yossel moved to New York. The two couples left Wisconsin because wages were higher in New York, and they thought they could save the money they needed to pay for their trip to Palestine more quickly. Both Regina and Golda were firmly set on going to Palestine; Yossel and Morris were both reluctantly following the women they loved. The four friends rented a six-room apartment in the city along with a Jewish Canadian couple also planning to immigrate. Morris quickly found work as a sign painter, Regina took a job as a secretary, Yossel became a barber, and Golda once again became a librarian. As soon as she reached New York, Meir immersed herself in Zionist activities. Her first job for the New York branch of the Poale Zion was sweeping floors at the organization's office. While quite different from delivering rousing speeches in Milwaukee, Meir did whatever work the organization gave her.

Though in time many of her friends abandoned their plans, Meir's commitment to going to Palestine only intensified. It was a hard decision to make. Those who decided to go were leaving their friends and families far behind and traveling to live in a country filled with danger and hardships. Many of the immigrants knew they would never see loved ones in the United States again. But for Meir there was no wavering. She had made her decision before she turned eighteen years old and she refused to change her mind.

Sad Farewells

By the spring of 1921, Golda and Morris finally had enough money to book passage on a ship bound for Palestine. Before leaving, they returned home to say good-bye to their families.

First they traveled to Philadelphia, where Morris's mother and three sisters lived, then to Milwaukee to Golda's family. Blume and Moshe tearfully bade their daughter good-bye and promised to move to Palestine as soon as they could afford to. Whenever that move took place, Golda's younger sister, Clara, would not be going with them. Clara had grown up in the United States and had no desire to leave. She was a student at the University of Wisconsin and loved her life in America. Meir knew that when she kissed Clara good-bye she might never see her sister again. But still she was determined to go. After Mil-

We Will Stay

Many of the new immigrants found life in Palestine too hard, but Golda was determined to stay. She told her brother-in-law so, and encouraged him to join her. This excerpt is from Ralph Martin's Golda Meir.

"Those who talk of returning are recent arrivals. An old worker is full of inspiration and faith. I say that as long as those who created the little that is here are here, I cannot leave, and you must come. I would not say this if I did not know that you are ready to work hard. True, even hard work is hard to find, but I have no doubt that you will find something. . . . If one wants one's own land, and if one wants it with one's whole heart, one must be ready for this. When you come, I am sure we will be able to plan. Perhaps you will come with us to Merhavia. Get ready. There is nothing to wait for."

waukee, it was on to Denver to say farewell to Shana and Sam, a trip that Golda was dreading. She knew that leaving Shana would be one of the hardest things she had ever done.

But Colorado held a surprise for Golda and Morris. During the visit, Shana besieged them with questions about their plans and what awaited the immigrants in Palestine. After days of Shana's endless questions, Sam teasingly asked his wife if she wanted to immigrate, too. To everyone's surprise, her answer was yes. Shana wanted to travel to Palestine with Morris and Golda. Over the next few days, Shana proved that she had thought the decision through long before Golda arrived. She described her plans carefully: She would take the two children—Judy, ten, and Chaim, three—and Sam would stay behind and send money to the family. Once she was settled in Palestine, then Sam would follow his family. Meir was flabbergasted, but excited. Now her husband, her best friend, Regina, and her favorite sister would be traveling with her. Shana's decision made leaving the United States much easier for Golda. She and Morris returned to New York and made their final plans, and Shana and the children arrived days before their ship was to depart.

In those final days, ominous news of Arab riots in Palestine began to trickle back to New York. The Arab citizens wanted to stop the influx of Jewish immigrants and the protests were turning bloody. Meir's friends begged her to stay, at least until it was safer. But she refused to listen. Her plans were made and she was going. On May 23, 1921, Meir's group of 22 immigrants set sail aboard the SS *Pocahontas*. Meir's group was a small part of the 9,140 immigrants who moved to Palestine

that year. Their route would take them to Naples, Italy, and then on to Palestine via Egypt. What seemed like a long but straightforward trip began as a nightmare. The ship's crew went on strike, claiming the vessel was not seaworthy, and the strike turned into a riot. Even after the violence was quelled and they set sail, tension was still high onboard. The ship took a week to sail from New York to Boston and once in Boston harbor the ship had to remain docked while the captain replaced most of his crew. Meir later described her trip:

> It had taken us three years to obtain money for tickets, but finally the day arrived—May 23, 1921—when we boarded a small, decrepit ship bound for Naples, the first leg on our way to Palestine. We were a small group, young, full of hope and zeal, ready for anything. We were all looking forward to the wonderful prospect of an ocean voyage, but right from the start it turned into a nightmare. First, we couldn't sail because of a strike. Then we spent nine days in Boston harbor, and our Zionist friends came up from New York and kissed us good-bye every day. The crew, still in a strike mood, had mutinied, and the engines broke down. . . . Many of our group left us in Boston, but the rest of us were not to be put off by mutinies or sabotaged machinery.[41]

The ship proved to be a problem throughout the voyage. Fires broke out, the engine room flooded, the pumps broke, and sailors were imprisoned for threatening to mutiny. Once in Naples, the immigrants had to find another ship to take them to Egypt. When the group finally arrived in Alexandria, they boarded a train for an overnight trip to Palestine. It was July and the train was hot, dusty, and crowded. There was no drinking water on-board and everyone was soon coated with dust. But Meir was thrilled and throughout the night the exhausted group broke into spontaneous song, singing about the life they imagined in Palestine. The group finally arrived at the Tel Aviv railroad station on July 14, 1921, two months after the journey had begun. The town looked hot, dusty, and deserted.

In her autobiography, Meir wrote of her first glimpse of Tel Aviv:

Although Tel Aviv looked to me like a large and not very attractive village on that scorching July morning when I first saw it through the filthy windows of the train . . . it was, in fact, already well on its way to becoming the world's youngest city. . . . I don't know what I had expected it to look like, but I certainly was not at all prepared for what I saw.[42]

What Meir saw was a city struggling to absorb a flood of immigrants from around the world. As Meir described it in her autobiography, whole sections of the city were unplanned, unfinished, and dirty. Exhausted and overwhelmed by their trip, Meir's group made their way to the only hotel in town. Even Meir, who had resolved to be a stoic immigrant, was horrified to find

An early Jewish settlement in Palestine. Despite the arduous journey to Palestine, many Jewish immigrants returned to their countries of origin, unable to cope with the hardships of their new homeland.

Arabs inspect goats for sale at a Jerusalem market in this circa 1925 photograph. Although other immigrants were appalled by the way of life in Palestine, Golda refused to be deterred.

their hotel rooms filled with bedbugs. Shana went to the market to buy meat and came back reporting that goods there were covered with flies and left to rot in the sun. That night the group had dinner with an American family they knew who had immigrated earlier. The family informed them that life in Palestine was too hard—they were giving up and returning to America.

Meir knew that life in Palestine was going to be hard, but she was determined to stay.

Golda, Morris, Shana, and the two children moved into a two-room apartment with an outside kitchen and a public toilet in the yard that was shared by forty people. Even these conditions did not stop Meir. She had come to Palestine to help build a Jewish nation, and that is what she did.

Chapter

5 Building a New Life

When Meir stepped off the train in Tel Aviv in 1921, she once more experienced the feeling of being a newcomer in an unfamiliar land. But unlike her childhood immigration to America, there was no waiting family to greet her and no home waiting to receive her. The life that awaited her this time included threats of violence from Arabs who vehemently opposed Jewish immigration, a hot, dry desert climate, and the daunting task of finding a place to live and a way to support her family.

Moving to a Kibbutz

Meir described her first few months in Palestine:

> We had to make our way alone in the land in which we had chosen to live. There was no State of Israel then, no Ministry of Absorption, no Jewish Agency. No one helped us settle or learn Hebrew or find a place to live. We had to do everything for ourselves, by ourselves, and it never occurred to us that anyone else was morally obligated to assist us. . . . We knew that it was up to each one of us personally to make our life in Palestine easier or better or more

meaningful and that we had no alternative other than to settle in and settle down as quickly as we possibly could.[43]

Settling in meant finding a job, which was not easy in a land flooded with immigrants. The only work Morris could find was a job as a bookkeeper for a British firm in Lydda. Even though it meant being separated from his wife, Morris took the job and commuted to Tel Aviv on weekends. Meir taught English to immigrants, a job she hated but kept because she needed the money. She had moved to Palestine to help build the Jewish nation of Israel, not to spread the English language. What Meir wanted to do was join a collective farm, called a kibbutz, and help build the country literally from the ground up.

On a kibbutz, everything is owned by the community and duties are shared. Members rotate jobs every week, men and women alike taking equal responsibility for everything from working on the farm to child care. The kibbutz was Meir's dream. Here she felt she could be a real pioneer and do the work of nation building.

Shana and Regina decided to stay in Tel Aviv, but Golda applied for membership in Kibbutz Merhavia, which was located in swampland in the Emek region of northern Palestine, southeast of the port

Kibbutz Nir David, a fertile oasis in the Jezreel Valley, was one of the many early Jewish settlements in Palestine.

city of Haifa. To Meir's astonishment, her application was rejected. The kibbutz leaders thought that Meir's life in America had not prepared her for the hard life on the farm. In her autobiography, Meir wrote:

> The group, which was made up at the time of about seven women and thirty men, couldn't imagine that an "American" girl either could or would do the extremely tough physical work that was required. Since many of the members had come from the States, they regarded themselves, understandably I suppose, as experts on everything American, including the character and

capabilities of an "American" girl like myself. . . . I felt as though [I had to prove] that even though I had lived in the States, I was still perfectly capable of doing a hard day's work. I argued fiercely that no one had the right to make such assumptions and that it was only fair to give us a chance to show what we could do.[44]

Hard Work and Adjustments

Determined to be part of the kibbutz, Meir applied a second time and was rejected

Women from Kibbutz Nahalal prepare the ground for crops in this 1936 photograph. The pioneers who built the first Jewish settlements in Palestine spent endless hours engaged in physical labor.

again. Along with her third application, Meir lodged a loud protest of the kibbutz's earlier decisions and demanded a trial period. The group agreed to allow Morris and Golda a one-month trial period before voting on their membership.

Meir was prepared for hardship and hard work, but even for her, life on the kibbutz was an adjustment. When they arrived in September 1921, the kibbutz consisted mostly of a few shacks and lots of mud and rocks. Merhavia's residents set out to drain the swamp and create a profitable farm. Meir described her early days clearing land at Kibbutz Merhavia. At the end of

the day, "the weight of a fork seemed a ton. I forced myself to eat, even though it was hard to look at, let alone swallow." [45] The work was hard, but Golda thrived, and at the end of the month she and Morris became official members.

But while Golda was overjoyed with life on the kibbutz, Morris was miserable. The lack of privacy and the lack of possessions were a great hardship for Morris. An intensely private man, Morris suddenly found himself forced to share everything. Even the clothes he wore were no longer his own. At the kibbutz, clothes were washed at the central laundry and distributed to all members. The shirt Morris wore one day might be worn by someone else the next.

While Morris tried to adjust, Golda immersed herself in the kibbutz and gradually into Zionist politics again. Because of her outspokenness, members of Merhavia selected her to represent them at the first kibbutz convention in 1922. Her speeches were rousing and brought her to the attention of the Zionist leaders David Ben-Gurion and Yitzhak Ben-Zvi. The two saw in Meir the ideal Zionist leader: a woman

The Terror Increases

Clashes between Jewish immigrants and Arabs increased in the years leading up to World War II. In her autobiography, Golda wrote about the fear that all Jewish settlers lived with daily.

"The riots started in April, 1936. By the summer it was no longer safe for Jews to travel from one city to another. Whenever I had to go from Tel Aviv to Jerusalem for a meeting—which was frequently—I kissed the children good-bye in the morning knowing that I might well never come home again, that my bus might be ambushed, that I might be shot by an Arab sniper at the entrance to Jerusalem, or stoned to death by an Arab mob on the outskirts of Tel Aviv. The Haganah [the underground Jewish self-defense organization] was much better equipped and larger than it had been at the time of the Arab riots of 1929, but we had no intention either of turning it into an instrument of counterterror against the Arabs just because they were Arabs or of providing the British with any excuse for further clamping down on Jewish immigration and settlement, as they tended to do whenever we visibly played too active a role in our own defense. Although it is always much harder to exercise self-restraint than it is to hit back, we had one paramount consideration: Nothing must be done—even in the face of constant danger and harassment—that might provoke the British into slashing the number of Jews allowed to enter Palestine. The policy of self-restraint (*havlagah* in Hebrew) was rigidly enforced. Whenever and wherever possible, Jews defended themselves from attack, but there were virtually no acts of retaliation by the Haganah throughout the three years of what the British, with splendid understatement, chose to call 'the disturbances.'"

of great intelligence and passion who also had a connection to America. She represented a valuable asset to the growing Zionist community.

Meir's exuberant speeches also impressed leaders of the Pioneer Women, a worldwide Zionist women's organization that provided social welfare services for Jewish women and children in Palestine. The Pioneer Women asked her to represent the organization in meetings with foreign dignitaries. Meir performed these duties well, impressing all those who observed her work and ultimately winning a place on an important managerial committee of the kibbutz.

Golda's activities left her less time to spend with Morris, who had become increasingly unhappy on the kibbutz. The matter finally reached a crisis point in 1924 when Morris contracted malaria and had to be hospitalized. The doctor was adamant; Morris could not return to the kibbutz. Life there was too strenuous for him. Faced with a choice between her personal life and her political convictions, Golda chose in favor of Morris. She left the kibbutz and returned with Morris to Tel Aviv.

Later, in her autobiography, Meir described her feelings on leaving Merhavia.

We packed up again—for the third time in three years—and made our farewells. It was a great wrench for me to leave the kibbutz, but I consoled myself tearfully by hoping that we would both be back soon, that Morris would regain his health quickly, that we would have a baby and that the relationship between us—which had so deteriorated in Merhavia—would improve. If all this happened, I told myself, then leaving the kibbutz for a while was a very small

price to pay. Unfortunately, it didn't work out that way.[46]

The departure from Merhavia began the worst period of Meir's life. She was not only leaving the kibbutz, but she was totally cutting herself off from politics, devoting herself to nursing Morris back to health and to becoming the kind of wife he wanted. But, Meir knew, to do this she would have to turn her back on politics and the Zionist cause.

Back to City Life

When the couple returned to Tel Aviv, Meir once again had to look for a job and a place to live. Work was scarce, and at first Golda had to live with Shana's family. Eventually she found a job as a cashier at the Histadrut's (Jewish Labor Federation) Public Works and Building Office. Morris was still too sick to work, so it was up to Golda to earn enough money to live on. Poverty and hunger were constants in her life during this time. Her days were filled with worry about having enough money for food and a place to live, about Morris's health, and about their future.

Tension eased a little when Morris's strength returned and a friend of Golda's offered him a job at the Jerusalem branch of the Public Works Department. The couple moved to Jerusalem, and with more money coming in and an apartment of their own they decided it was time to start a family. In November 1924, Golda gave birth to their son, Menachem. A little less than two years later, in May 1926, their daughter, Sarah, was born. Reaffirming the commitment she had made on leaving

A Certain Type of Woman

Meir's hiatus from public life left her unhappy and unfulfilled. She describes her own needs in objective terms in Israel and Mary Shenker's As Good as Golda.

"There is a type of woman who cannot remain at home. In spite of the place her children and her family fill in her life, her nature demands something more; she cannot divorce herself from the larger social life. She cannot let her children narrow her horizon. For such a woman, there is no rest."

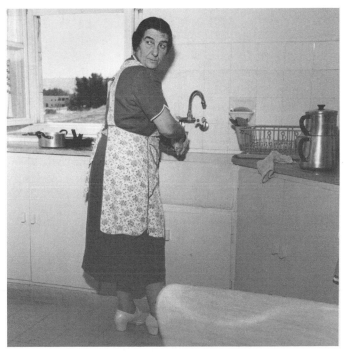

Golda works in a kitchen in Israel in 1956. Meir had a difficult time being a wife and mother as she longed to be involved in the larger world around her.

the kibbutz, Golda vowed to be the kind of wife and mother that would make Morris happy. She desperately tried to honor her vow, but her decision to turn her back on the Zionist cause left her wretched:

All these hopes and good intentions notwithstanding, instead of the placid domestic life that I now told myself I was ready to accept, the four years that we lived in Jerusalem were the most miserable I ever experienced. . . . Almost everything went wrong: sometimes I even felt that I was reliving the worst part of my mother's life, and I used to remember . . . the stories she told us about the years when she and Father were so terribly poor in Russia. . . . But it wasn't only our actual poverty—or even my constant fear that my children would be hungry—that made me so wretched. There was also my loneliness, the sense of isolation to which I was so unaccustomed and the constant feeling that I was being deprived of just those things for which I had come to Palestine in the first place. Instead of actively helping build the Jewish national home and working hard and productively for it, I found myself cooped up in a tiny apartment in Jerusalem, all my thoughts and energy concentrated on making do with Morris's wages.[47]

Finally the years of frustration, poverty, and bitterness ended when Meir ran into her old friend David Remez, one of the leaders of the Zionist movement. Remez was surprised by the changes in Meir. Gone was the vibrant and dynamic revolutionary that Meir once was, and in her place was a worried and frustrated woman who felt trapped by her life. Seeing how miserable Meir was, Remez offered her a job as secretary of the Moetzet Hapoalot, the Women's Labor Council. The council was in charge of teaching agriculture and trade skills to women immigrants and tutoring them in Hebrew, the language of their new homeland. The job would be a struggle and a challenge, Remez told Meir, involving long hours, much travel, and protracted periods away from her family.

But these hardships would be offset with the knowledge that she was once again working to build a Jewish homeland. Meir enthusiastically accepted the position.

This decision marked the end of Meir's isolation and the beginning of her climb to political power. It also marked the end of Meir's marriage. Morris remained in Jerusalem when Golda moved to Tel Aviv with the children. Though they never divorced, and they remained friendly for the rest of their lives, the couple never lived together again. Morris remained close to his family and later described the reason he and Golda separated by saying, "I came to Palestine for one reason only. To be with Goldie. But she was never there."[48]

Meir never spoke publicly about her separation from Morris. Friends later said that she continued to love her estranged husband but that her dedication to the Jewish homeland outweighed her dedication to her marriage.

The Personal Price of Political Involvement

In her autobiography, Meir wrote about her work with the Women's Council:

I have had a great regard for those energetic hardworking women in the ranks of the labor movement . . . who succeeded in equipping dozens of city-bred girls with the sort of theoretical knowledge and a sound practical training that made it possible for them to do their share (and often much more than their share) of the work going on in the agricultural settlements throughout

Palestine. That kind of constructive feminism really does women credit and matters much more than who sweeps the house or who sets the table.[49]

The role of Jewish women in Palestine was one of equality. Women struggled alongside male workers digging ditches, paving roads, and helping build the country. For many of the immigrants, it was a struggle to balance their new lives with the traditional roles most had grown up with. When Meir returned to Tel Aviv and her active political life, she also found herself struggling with the dual roles of home and career life. This struggle was to remain a central theme throughout her life.

Later, Meir described her feelings in an article she wrote for *The Ploughwoman*, a

A Lonely Struggle

In an anonymous article, excerpted in Peggy Mann's Golda, *Golda wrote about her lonely battle to balance life as a mother and as an active member of the new Israeli government.*

"Taken as a whole, the inner struggles and the despair of the mother who goes to work are without parallel in human experience. . . . There are some mothers who work only when they are forced to, when the husband is sick or unemployed. In such cases the mother feels her course of action is justified. . . . But there is a type of woman who cannot remain at home for other reasons. . . . She cannot divorce herself from the larger social life. . . . And for such a woman, there is no rest.

Theoretically it looks straightforward enough. The woman who replaces her with the children is devoted, loves the children, is reliable and suited to the work; the children are fully looked after. . . . She, of course, has the great advantage of being able to develop. . . . Therefore she can bring more to her children than if she were to remain at home. Everything looks all right. But one look of reproach from the little one when the mother goes away and leaves it with the stranger is enough to throw down the whole structure of vindication. That look, that plea to the mother to stay, can be withstood only by an almost superhuman effort of the will. . . .

This eternal inner division, this double pull, this alternating feeling of unfulfilled duty—today toward her family, the next day toward her work—this is the burden of the working mother."

collection of essays written by the early immigrants to Palestine:

> Your heart is rent. . . . A mother in public life—in her feelings—will never be the same as a man or a father in public life. . . . When the mother has to leave home in the morning for work and the child [has] a temperature, even if the best person is taking care, it is not the same. She leaves it in the morning with a temperature. She comes back in the evening; it's still sick, but she worries about her work. Or she's tired. Fathers also worry—I don't believe that mothers love their children more than fathers, that is nonsense—but there is something different there.[50]

Meir's children also struggled with their feelings about their mother's absence during their early childhood. Sarah later described these years to one of Meir's biographers:

Golda poses with her son, Menachem (left), and his family. When her children were young, Golda struggled with her desire to maintain a strong connection to her family while at the same time yearning to be involved in politics.

Mother traveled all over. . . . Sometimes weeks would pass and we didn't see each other. My brother suffered a great deal from this and he often gave vent to his protests. He quarreled with Mother and tried to stop her from leaving the house to go to meetings. I was more tolerant, but I also felt lonely without her. We were always lonesome for Mother because we saw very little of her.[51]

However, Meir was committed to helping build a Jewish state no matter the personal sacrifice. As always, Meir threw herself into her work. She traveled across Palestine overseeing the council's projects, spent hours in countless fund-raising projects, and traveled endlessly both in Palestine and abroad carrying the message of the council. Throughout 1929 and 1930 Meir traveled to England and the United States to raise support and funds for Jewish immigrants. Each time she was gone several weeks, and each time she felt torn between her duties to her country and her obligations to her family. But, for Meir, her country came first.

While the decision was the only one Meir felt she could make, she still felt guilty. And at times, she felt that her family suffered from her work. In her autobiography, Meir wrote that her own life was an

illustration of these dilemmas and difficulties [facing all women in Palestine]. I was always rushing from one place to another—to work, home, to a meeting, to take Menachem to a music lesson, to keep a doctor's appointment with Sarah, to shop, to cook, to work and back home again. And still to this day I am not sure that I didn't harm the children or neglect them, despite the efforts I made not to be away from them even an hour more than was strictly necessary. They grew up to be healthy, productive, talented and good people, and they both are wonderful parents to their own children and wonderful companions to me. But when they were growing up, I knew that they deeply resented my activities outside the home.[52]

Indeed, Meir's choices were hard on her children. But Meir could not turn away from her dedication to building a homeland for the Jewish people.

6 The Birth of a Nation

As Meir struggled to balance her roles as mother and political leader, she also found herself thrust into a new role—that of a warrior. Meir found herself fighting pitched political battles against the British government, against immigration policies that were condemning European Jews to death, and finally against the staggering odds of bringing forth a vital Jewish nation amidst a host of Arab countries that rejected its formation. This was the beginning of the most challenging, but most rewarding, time of Meir's life.

Let Them Come to Palestine

Adolf Hitler came to power in Germany in January 1933, promising prosperity for the German people. He also vowed to rid his country (and the world) of Jews, whom he blamed for Germany's political, financial, and social problems. Over the next three years, 150,000 Jews fled Europe and arrived in Palestine. Alarmed by the growing Jewish immigration, Arabs in Palestine and in the surrounding Arab countries responded with organized protests and violence.

While the Arab states protested that the number of immigrants coming to Palestine was too high, Meir and other Jewish leaders loudly proclaimed that it was too low. In 1938 Meir attended an international conference on refugees in France as the official Jewish observer from Palestine. For months before the conference, Meir had been gathering information about persecution of Jews in Germany and surrounding regions. Meir attended the conference to plead for unlimited Jewish emigration from Germany.

Her speech to the conference was simple and direct. If the rest of the world would not help the immigrants, then the Jews in Palestine were ready to absorb them. "We have little bread," Meir said; "however, we will share the crumbs of that bread with them."[53] But Meir's pleas fell on deaf ears. No one would commit to helping the Jews leave Europe. Nor would any country support the idea of unlimited Jewish immigration to Palestine. Meir's reception at the conference convinced her more strongly than ever that the Jewish people must have their own independent homeland. If the Jews had an independent nation, then they could offer sanctuary without pleading for international help. Meir returned to Palestine determined to fight for a Jewish homeland and to fight for the lives of the European Jews.

Adolf Hitler came to power promising to rid Germany of its Jewish population. In response, many Jews fled Germany for Palestine.

The British White Paper

On her return, Meir encountered a new and unexpected foe: the British government. Looking for ways to end turmoil in the region, the British government issued a White Paper in May 1939 calling for the creation of an Arab-Jewish binational state within a ten-year period. The paper stated that Jewish immigration to Palestine would be limited to seventy-five thousand refugees a year for a five-year period. At the end of the fifth year, all Jewish immigration to the area would be prohibited unless approved by Palestine's Arab population.

This White Paper marked the end of British support for the Jewish state promised in the Balfour Declaration, and many Jewish leaders thought it was the end of their dreams for a Jewish nation. As Amos Perlmutter, a professor of government, wrote in *Israel: The Partitioned State:*

The issuance of the 1939 British White Paper in the wake of the Arab Revolt was a clear sign that the [government] was no longer making any pretense of supporting the Balfour Declaration, that it was clearly tilting towards the Arabs while abandoning and becoming hostile to Zionism and its aspirations, and was bent on curtailing any drive toward a Jewish commonwealth or Jewish statehood.[54]

The British stance on limiting Jewish immigration to Palestine at a time of desperation for European Jews was seen by Zionist leaders as a terrible betrayal. Nevertheless, the Jews of Palestine fought beside Great Britain and the other Allied nations in the war against Nazi Germany.

At the same time, they continued their political battle against the edicts laid down in the White Paper. As David Ben-Gurion stated, "We shall fight with Great Britain in this war as if there was no White Paper and we shall fight the White Paper as if there was no war."[55]

World War II

During the war, Meir served on the War Economic Advisory Council as a liaison be-

Buildings in London crumble to the ground as Germany relentlessly bombs the city. Jews in Palestine fought alongside British and Allied soldiers during World War II.

Israel's Defenders

Support for the Haganah, the underground Jewish defense force, grew during World War II. On June 18, 1947, David Ben-Gurion wrote a statement on the existence of the Haganah. The following is excerpted from Ben-Gurion's Israel: A Personal History.

"Its task was the *defense of Jewish settlements* against Arab attacks, not by individuals but by bands incited and organized by a *central Arab political body.* . . . Arab aggression is a different matter. There the Hagana is the most important, indeed the decisive factor. An armed attack by the Arabs can only be stopped by Jewish military might. . . . Our most crucial task now is to prepare the Hagana to meet this challenge, to defend successfully not only Jewish settlements and the [Jewish community] as a whole, but in time of need to defend the entire Land of Israel and our whole national future."

Haganah members in Jerusalem defend their positions near the King David Hotel in 1948. To protect their homeland, Jews in Palestine had to have an effective military.

tween the Jewish public in Palestine and the British administration. Meir's job included improving production and distribution of goods inside of Palestine, negotiating with the British to improve the wages of the Jewish civilians working on military projects, and increasing British protection of Palestine's Jews from Arab attacks.

While these were her council duties, Meir's unofficial goal during the war was to help European Jews escape their war-torn countries and immigrate to Palestine.

Demonstrators in Palestine protest on the anniversary of Britain's issuance of the White Paper, which limited Jewish immigration into Palestine.

That goal became an imperative in November 1942 when a group of Jews from Poland brought news of the Nazi persecution of the Jews and Hitler's call for mass annihilation. Meir and other Jewish leaders became frantic to save as many European Jews as possible. When the British government refused to increase quotas, the Jewish Executive Committee began looking for illegal means to help immigrants escape Europe and journey to Palestine. In her autobiography, Meir wrote how she felt about the immigrants who had survived the concentration camps and later journeyed to Palestine:

> I remember listening to the people who gave evidence and wondering how and where they found the will to live, to rear new families, to become human beings once more. I suppose the answer is that all of us, finally, crave life—regardless of what the past has held—but just as I cannot really know what it was like in the death camps, so I cannot really ever know what it was like to start all over again. That knowledge belongs to the survivors.[56]

To enable survivors to reach Palestine, Meir helped buy ships to transport the immigrants illegally. She worked with Haganah, an underground Jewish defense force, to equip resistance fighters to sneak into German-occupied territories and establish routes to transport refugees out. Many of the European Jews were successfully smuggled into Palestine. Those who were caught were either deported or allowed to remain and their numbers subtracted from the number of immigrants allowed to enter legally that month. Jewish voices around the world denounced the immigration quotas. The Jewish Agency stated that the policy was "devoid of any moral justification. . . . It is not the Jewish refugees returning to their homeland who are violating the law, but those who are endeavoring to deprive them of the supreme right of every human being—the right to live."[57]

A Vow to Create a Jewish Homeland

The Jewish Agency's words proved to be prophetic: At the end of the war, the world reacted with shock to evidence of the Nazi concentration camps and the murder of six million Jews. Never again, vowed the Jews of Palestine, would this be allowed to happen. There would be a Jewish state and a refuge for all who sought to enter. In her autobiography, Meir wrote that "in the final analysis, it was the Jews of Europe, trapped, doomed and destroyed, who taught us once and for all that we must become the masters of our own undertaking."[58]

Many European Jews who survived the war chose to immigrate to Palestine. In the months following the end of the war in May 1945, an estimated one hundred thousand Jewish refugees were in refugee camps waiting to flee Europe. Meir, and Jewish leaders around the world, called for the refugees to be sent to Palestine immediately. But their pleas were denied. The British government did not want to anger the Arab nations who continued to oppose

Golda wanted to offer Jews who had survived the German concentration camps (pictured) illegal passage to Israel. At the end of the war, as many as one hundred thousand Jewish refugees were waiting to immigrate to Palestine.

Jewish immigration and a Jewish state in their midst. Faced with Britain's refusal to open the door to Jewish immigration, Meir and other Jewish leaders began a covert rebellion against Great Britain.

Rebellion

The fight was carried out by members of Haganah, many of whom had received their military training from the British government. During the war, fearing that Germany might sweep into the area and establish a foothold in the Middle East, Great Britain began training a Jewish militia. A training school was set up where Jewish volunteers received instruction in sabotage, demolition, and tactical warfare. The training they received during the war made it possible for the immigrants to fight for the establishment of a Jewish state following the war. Meir and her two children

The Final Solution

In 1942 Adolf Hitler called for the "final solution of the Jewish question," the extermination of European Jewry. In a speech, Meir summed up the chilling human statistics of Hitler's plan. The following is excerpted from Peggy Mann's Golda.

"Hitler did not solve the Jewish Question according to his plans. But he did annihilate six million Jews—Jews of Germany, France, Belgium, Holland, Luxembourg, Poland, the USSR, Hungary, Yugoslavia, Greece, Italy, Czechoslovakia, Austria, Rumania. With these Jews there were destroyed over thirty thousand Jewish communities which for centuries had been the center of Jewish faith, learning, and scholarship. From this Jewry stemmed some of the giants in the fields of arts, literature, and science. Was it only this generation of Jews that was gassed? *One million children*—the future generation—were annihilated. Who can encompass this picture in all its horror and its consequences for the Jewish people for many generations to come?

And what about those who remained alive? Who are they? Each individual is a splinter of a family destroyed—each one lives in the nightmare recollection of his dearest and closest led to the crematorium. Mothers who have seen their babies thrown into the air and used as targets for Nazi bullets. Thousands upon thousands of Jewish women who will never be mothers because of the Nazi 'scientific experiments' performed on them. . . . All victims of the attempt to solve the Jewish Question."

British soldiers in Israel deport illegal immigrants in 1946. Golda worked with the Haganah to sabotage British efforts to control Jewish immigration to Israel.

were all members of Haganah, even though they kept their membership secret from one another and never discussed their involvement in the movement. Meir feared for Menachem and Sarah's safety, but never forbade them to participate in the militia's activities. Like her, her high-school-age children were fighting for a Jewish state. In her autobiography, Meir wrote:

> Both the children, like nearly all the teenagers . . . were involved in Haganah activities, although the subject

was never openly discussed at home. But even if they said nothing, parents and schoolteachers knew that youngsters had often been up late serving as couriers for the underground or circulating Haganah posters and leaflets. I remember actually writing one of those posters myself at home, although of course I took great care not to let the children see what I was doing. A day or two afterward Sarah said, . . . "I'll be back late tonight, maybe even very late." Naturally I wanted to know why. "I can't tell you," she said, and walked off with a parcel under her arm. I knew perfectly well what was in that parcel, and I also knew that pasting up "illegal" posters was a very risky business in those days. I stayed awake till dawn that night waiting for her to come home: but we observed all the rules, and I didn't as much touch on the subject the next morning, although I was dying to say something.[59]

Like all of the Jewish political leaders in Palestine, Meir had some involvement in Haganah's efforts to buy arms and resist British opposition to Jewish immigration. Meir also helped organize the smuggling of Jewish immigrants into Palestine. In her autobiography, she later wrote that of all of her work with Haganah, that which she did to help bring European Jews into Palestine, and seeing her own children involved in the work, was the most rewarding: "One miracle was that the Jews still came, in the face of the British gas bombs and truncheons, knowing that some might be killed and that all would be shipped off to detention in Cyprus. But the other miracle was that our own children were with us in the struggle."[60]

Resistance Escalates

Meir watched the danger increase as Haganah resistance fighters moved from nonviolent to violent tactics. Britain did not change its immigration policy and on October 1, 1945, Haganah began conducting acts of sabotage against the British in Palestine. On October 31, the Palestine railway system was blown up in 153 places and Haganah vowed to continue until the refugees were allowed to enter Palestine.

The British government appointed a committee to study the problem, and Meir was one of the Jewish leaders called to testify. On March 25, 1946, she told the panel:

> I am authorized, on behalf of the close to one hundred and sixty thousand members of the Histadrut to state here in the clearest terms that there is nothing that Jewish labor is not prepared to do in this country in order to receive large masses of Jewish immigrants, with no limitations and with no conditions whatsoever.[61]

While the committee gathered testimony, guerrilla actions increased and the British government tightened control, issuing emergency regulations for the area that amounted to martial law. In protest, Meir called for a hunger strike. She met with the Jewish National Council, which decided that the strike would be confined to fifteen people in good health. Meir desperately wanted to participate, but she had been severely ill and her doctor warned her against it. Meir ignored her doctor's warning, declaring that whether she was with the other official protesters or at home by herself, she would fast. Meir joined the protesters. They fasted for 101 hours, until two boatloads of immigrants detained in Europe were allowed to sail for Palestine and the 1,014 people onboard were issued immigration certificates.

The same month of Meir's fast, May 1946, the British government's study committee finally released its report. The committee recommended the immediate admission of all one hundred thousand Jews waiting to enter the area as an effort to bring peace to Palestine. But the British government refused to heed both the advice of its own committee and mounting public pressure. Jewish immigration would continue as before and the refugees would remain in their camps. The government felt that unrestricted Jewish immigration would provoke a violent reaction among Arab nations. Britain feared that foreign powers like the Soviet Union would use the turmoil to increase their presence in the region. In response, Meir called for plans for massive civil disobedience against the British government. Meir wanted the World Zionist Organization to call for massive demonstrations against the British government by Jews around the world and for intensive demonstrations in Palestine. Her plans failed when some leaders of the Jewish Executive Committee refused to call for widespread acts of civil disobedience.

The Birth of a Nation

Though there was no official call for open rebellion, violence continued to escalate. At this time, Meir was head of the Political Department of the Jewish Agency. Her job was to fulfill the orders of the Jewish Executive Committee, and she found herself doing everything from working with Haganah volunteers to bartering for armaments. She also was responsible for explaining Judaism and the importance of a Jewish homeland to the world. When a commission of the recently created United Nations came to Palestine in 1947, it was Meir's job to escort its members through Palestine and convince them of the need for a Jewish nation. Meir later reported: "It could be said with certainty that when the eleven members of the United Nations Special Commission reached this country, there wasn't one among them who knew Palestinian affairs before he was appointed to the Commission."[62] It was Meir's job to make sure they understood. Her duties took her across Palestine; often she faced sniper gunfire, the threat of attack from Arab residents, and confrontations with British soldiers who policed the area. During this time, Meir often traveled with an armed guard, but she refused to quit traveling. Her duties to the Jewish state were more important than her personal safety.

Finally, in 1947, unable to resolve the regional conflict, Great Britain decided to

"Pure as the Sun of Palestine"

As World War II continued, even young children worked to help the European refugees enter Palestine. Meir was proud of the children, including her son and daughter, who risked their lives to bring the refugees into Palestine. The following is excerpted from My Life.

"The time came when the [children] themselves gave us the answer. They are strangers to casuistry and abstract precepts. They are plain and pure as the sun of Palestine. For them, matters are simple, clear and uncomplicated. When the catastrophe descended upon the Jews of the world, and Jews began coming to Palestine in 'illegal' ships, as they still do, we saw these children of ours go down to the seas and risk their lives—this is no rhetoric, but literally so—to ford the waves and reach the boats and bear the Jews ashore on their shoulders. This, too, is no rhetoric, no flowery speech, but the literal truth: sixteen- and eighteen-year-old Palestinian girls and boys carried the survivors on their backs. From the mouths of Jews borne on those shoulders I have heard how they shed tears for the first time—after all they had been through in Europe for seven years—when they saw Palestinian youngsters bearing grown men and women to the soil of the homeland. We have been blessed in this youth, which sets out to offer its life not on behalf of its own particular kibbutz, or [for] Palestine in general, but for the sake of every Jewish child, or old man, seeking entry."

call upon the United Nations for help. The government issued an official statement on February 18, 1947, announcing that "His Majesty's Government have of themselves no power . . . to award the country to the Arabs or the Jews, or even to partition it between them. . . . We have therefore reached the conclusion that the only course open to us is to submit the problem to the judgement of the United Nations."[63]

In response, the United Nations convened its first special session in April 1947 to deal with the issue of Palestine. An eleven-member study panel, the United Nations Special Committee on Palestine (UNSCOP), was formed to gather data and consider options; meanwhile, violence escalated throughout the summer. British soldiers were killed by Haganah guerrillas; in response, British troops in Tel Aviv went on a rampage, firing at buses and smashing cafés.

On August 31 UNSCOP issued a report recommending the end of British rule in Palestine and the partition of Palestine into an Arab state, a Jewish state, and an international zone containing the holy places in Jerusalem, revered by Jews, Muslims, and Christians alike. The Jews accepted the plan. The Arab League publicly condemned the report and refused to adopt any plan that created an official Jewish state. The British government also disliked UNSCOP's recommendations and refused to support any proposal unless it had approval of both the Arab nations and the Jewish settlers in Palestine. But in the face of vehement multiparty opposition, the United Nations officially adopted the plan on November 29, 1947. The partition resolution was endorsed by a vote of 33 to 13, supported by both the United States and the Soviet Union. The British abstained. Following the vote, Great Britain announced that it would withdraw from Palestine in May 1948 and that it would leave no troops in place to police the partition of Palestine.

In Palestine, Arab protests against partition erupted into violence, with attacks on Jewish settlements that promised full-scale war. The British refusal to intervene brought home to Meir the stark reality that soon Jewish Palestine would have to be totally self-reliant and must be able to defend its own borders. To do this, the new nation would have to raise money and buy weapons to defend itself after the British withdrawal.

"We Will Fight"

Once again Meir's fund-raising skills were put to the test. In January 1948, she was sent back to the United States to raise money from American Jews to buy arms. Her first speech was a totally impromptu plea before the General Assembly of the Council of Jewish Federations and Welfare Funds. Without notes, Meir spoke from her heart:

> The Jewish community in Palestine is going to fight to the very end. If we have arms to fight with, we will fight with them. If not, we will fight with stones in our hands. . . . There is no Jew in Palestine who does not believe that finally we will be victorious. That is the spirit of the country. . . . But this valiant spirit alone cannot face rifles and machine guns. . . . Spirit without arms can, in time, be broken together with the body.[64]

Her audience listened, wept, and contributed. During her six weeks in the United States, Meir raised fifty million dollars.

Jews celebrate the United Nations decision to end British rule and partition Palestine into an Arab state, a Jewish state, and an international zone.

Knowing that war was a virtual certainty if they proclaimed Jewish Palestine an independent state, members of the Executive Committee voted to proceed. In Tel Aviv on May 14, 1948, the Provisional State Council proclaimed the establishment of the Jewish State in Palestine. It would be called Medinat Israel (the State of Israel), and it would be open to Jews worldwide. Meir was one of the twenty-five signers of the proclamation giving birth to a new nation. Her cosigners were among the most influential people in the Jewish Zionist movement; all were to be members of the new provisional government that would lead Israel into existence. Meir was one of only two women in the group.

Meir wrote of her feelings that day as she watched the ceremony:

Whatever happened now, whatever price any of us would have to pay for it, we had re-created the Jewish national home. The long exile was over. From this day on we would no longer live on sufferance in the land of our forefathers. Now we were a nation like other nations, master—for the first time in twenty centuries—of our own destiny. The dream had come true.[65]

The new nation faced staggering odds, well summarized by the *New York Post:*

Imagine an area of 8,000 square miles in all. Make it 270 miles long and seventy miles wide at its widest; border it on three sides with enemy nations, their armies totaling between 70,000 and 80,000 troops; place within it 600,000 people from more than fifty nations, whose last experience with self-rule dates back 1,887 years; sever its sea and

air communications; besiege one-sixth of its number in a land-bound enclave; sack its former government; give it a name; declare it independent—and you have the State of Israel, one minute past midnight, May 15, 1948.[66]

Fighting for Survival

Israel's birth came one day before the British government's official control of Palestine expired. Eleven minutes after Britain's control ended, President Harry S Truman announced formal U.S. recognition of Israel; Guatemala and the Soviet Union quickly followed. Israel was a nation, and its existence had been recognized by two of the leading world powers. Celebrations broke out in the streets of Tel Aviv, and the new nation rejoiced.

But the exultation was short-lived. On May 15 the joint forces of Egypt, Jordan, Syria, Lebanon, and Iraq attacked Israeli territory. What had been viewed as civil war in Palestine became an international conflict now known as the first Arab-Israeli war. In Israel the conflict is called the War of Independence. Egyptian planes bombed Tel Aviv, and Ben-Gurion's first broadcast as prime minister of Israel was made from an air-raid shelter. The Executive Committee feared as many as sixty thousand casualties in the conflict, or one in ten Jewish immigrants. Even facing these odds, Israel was prepared to fight. "I don't think anyone can rationally explain it," Meir later said.

We would not ask for a state if we did not think we could defend ourselves. . . . Those who were killed in the gas chambers were the last Jews to die without de-

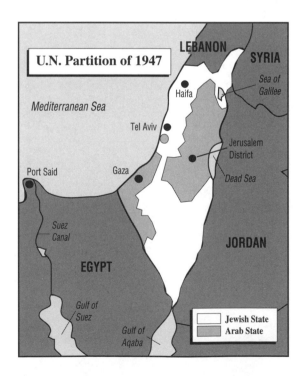

U.N. Partition of 1947

LEBANON

SYRIA

Sea of Galilee

Haifa

Mediterranean Sea

Tel Aviv

Jerusalem District

Port Said

Gaza

Dead Sea

Suez Canal

JORDAN

EGYPT

Gulf of Suez

Gulf of Aqaba

Jewish State
Arab State

Israeli troops take defensive positions in the Negev desert during the War of Independence.

fending themselves. . . . I didn't know how we would make it. . . . I only knew one thing, that we must. . . . We had a secret weapon: "No alternative!"[67]

In Israel's favor, the Arab armies were disorganized and lacked a central command. None of the Arab nations wanted to cede even temporary control of its army to another nation, so each army attacked independently. The Israelis, with no place to withdraw to and no ally nearby, fought desperately and managed to hold off the invading armies. Fighting continued until the UN Security Council intervened and called for a truce on May 29. The negotiated truce, agreed to by all warring parties, went into effect on June 11, 1948. With the UN-imposed peace, Israel had breathing room to establish itself as a nation.

Meir used this time to return to the United States to raise more money for her fledgling country. This was the first of many trips she would make for Israel. Once again Meir was forced to choose between her personal desires and the needs of her country. Once again she chose Israel:

For me to have to leave Israel at the moment the state was established was more difficult than I can say. The very last thing I wanted to do was go abroad [but] no one knew better than I what that kind of money would mean to Israel, how desperately we needed the arms it would buy. . . . My heart sank at the thought of tearing myself away from the country, but there was no real choice at all.[68]

7 Political Years

Meir's accomplishments already surpassed what most people would achieve in a lifetime. But her success up to this point would pale before the achievements of the next few years of her life. After Israel gained its independence, Meir was propelled to the forefront of the political scene as ambassador, foreign minister, and finally prime minister.

While still in the United States trying to raise funds for Israel, Meir received what was to be the first of many honors. She was offered the position of Israeli ambassador to Russia. But it was an honor that Meir desperately wanted to refuse. In her autobiography, Meir outlined her feelings when she received the telegram from Foreign Minister Moshe Sharrett offering her the position:

> The state was not even a month old. The war was not over. The children were not yet safe. I had a family and dear friends in Israel, and it seemed to me that it was grossly unfair to ask me to pack my bags again so soon and take off for such a remote and essentially unknown post. . . . There were plenty of other people who could do the job as well, better in fact. And Russia of all places, the country I had left as a little girl and of which I had not a single pleasant memory.[69]

But the post was offered with the approval of Prime Minister Ben-Gurion, and Meir knew she could not refuse the offer. As Meir said later, one's duty was one's duty, and Meir never shirked her duty. When numerous appeals did not change Ben-Gurion's decision, Meir accepted the post. She would leave the country she had worked so hard to help create and serve it from Russia.

Madam Ambassador

Fifty-year-old Meir arrived in Moscow on September 3, 1948, and with her staff of twenty-one Israelis took up residence in the Hotel Metropole, which was to serve as the first Israeli embassy. Funds were meager, so Meir decided to run the embassy like a kibbutz. Embassy employees drew no salaries; each person was given the same amount of spending money regardless of his or her job. Meir, along with her secretary, scoured the local open-air markets for inexpensive food, which members of her delegation were expected to cook on hot plates in their hotel rooms. When the Israelis moved into their own embassy, Meir helped hang the curtains and lay the carpet.

Golda Meir and her daughter leave for Russia, where Meir was posted as the first Israeli ambassador.

One of Meir's chief goals in the Soviet Union was to contact Russian Jews to determine their status and welfare under Soviet rule. Judaism had been officially banned in Russia, Hebrew was a forbidden language for Russian citizens, and only a few synagogues remained open. Russian officials informed Meir that almost all Jews in Russia had been assimilated and now viewed themselves not as Jews but simply as Soviet citizens. When Meir attended services at Moscow's Great Synagogue, the official's words seemed to be true: At the time an estimated half million people of Jewish heritage lived in Moscow; Meir was amazed to find less than three hundred people in attendance.

A few weeks later, Meir attended services at the temple again to celebrate Rosh Hashanah, the Jewish New Year. In the weeks since her first visit, news of the Israeli ambassador's visit had spread by word of mouth. When Meir arrived this time,

she was amazed to find fifty thousand people crowding into and around the synagogue. The mass encircled her before she entered the building, crowding around her, calling her name, and reaching out to touch her. Over and over, the crowd shouted in Yiddish "*Goldele, leben sollst du. Shana tova,*" [70] or "Golda, long life to you. Happy New Year." To the crowd, she was the living symbol of the new Jewish nation. Meir was shaken, and later said, "I am sure that not only I, but everyone who was a member of this first mission, inwardly asked forgiveness a thousand times from these Jews for having dared to doubt their spiritual strength and their Jewish ties with the whole past, present, and future of the Jewish race." [71]

Knowing that Jews inside Russia hungered for information, Meir saw it as her duty to spread news of Israel whenever possible. The Israeli embassy began producing and distributing to local Russian

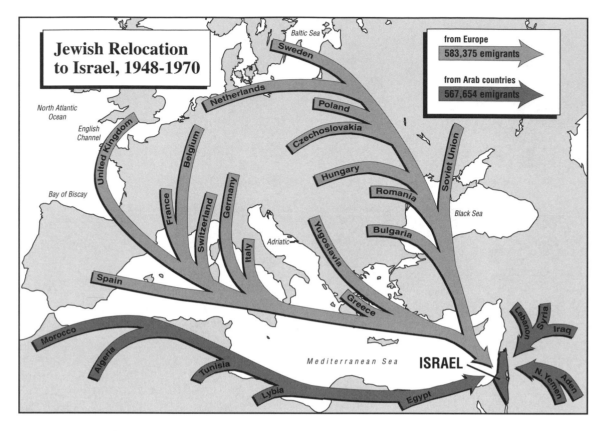

Jewish Relocation to Israel, 1948–1970

North Atlantic Ocean

English Channel

Bay of Biscay

Baltic Sea

from Europe
583,375 emigrants

from Arab countries
567,654 emigrants

Sweden
Netherlands
Poland
Czechoslovakia
United Kingdom
Belgium
Hungary
Soviet Union
France
Switzerland
Germany
Romania
Italy
Black Sea
Adriatic
Yugoslavia
Bulgaria
Spain
Greece
Lebanon
Syria
Iraq
Morocco
Mediterranean Sea
ISRAEL
Algeria
Tunisia
N. Yemen
Aden
Lybia
Egypt

groups a newsletter discussing Israel and current events in the country. Meir was immediately called into the office of the Soviet foreign minister, who informed her the newsletter was a serious breach of diplomatic etiquette and Soviet law.

News releases prepared by the Israeli diplomats were never published in Soviet newspapers, and news about Israel was always censored. Every initiative Meir suggested was rejected by the Soviets. The government refused to discuss arms deals or cultural exchanges with her and refused to even acknowledge the subject of the immigration of Soviet Jews to Israel. During this time, Meir often felt frustrated and ineffective. "One could send a dummy as minister and it would have the same impact,"[72] she said.

Finally, in February 1949, Prime Minister Ben-Gurion cabled Meir requesting that she return to Israel. Ben-Gurion's political party, the Mapai or Labor Party, had won the country's first elections and forty-six seats in the Knesset, the Israeli Parliament. Ben-Gurion wanted Meir to come home and become part of the newly elected government. Meir was overjoyed to be returning to her home and the work she loved. On March 11, 1949, Meir was sworn in as Israel's first minister of labor.

Minister of Labor

When Meir took office, she was faced with a staggering inflation rate, huge war debts, a lack of housing for Israeli citizens, and a serious unemployment problem. Soldiers who returned home from compulsory service often had to sleep on park benches because they could not find housing. The problem of feeding, housing, and absorbing the one thousand immigrants a day who were streaming into Israel also fell under the jurisdiction of Meir's ministry. After assessing her tasks, Meir issued her first order of business: Housing and jobs were to be the ministry's main focus. "For the most part, the new immigrants come destitute, many of them broken in body and spirit. They have to be fed, clothed, given a physical examination, their sanitation needs attended to, their sick cared for. They must be given food, shelter, a roof over their heads. All in one day, the first day. Afterwards, we need schools, hospitals, work, houses, especially houses."[73]

On May 24, 1950, Meir brought one of her most ambitious proposals to the Knesset for approval. Dubbed the Meyerson Plan (she had not yet changed her last name to the Hebrew Meir), the project called for building thirty thousand new housing units. With the Knesset's approval, and Meir's appeal to Jews around the world for funds, the housing units were built. At the time, Meir said of her plan, "I presented a project for which I don't have the money. In the meantime, we will be happy and [the immigrants] will be happy, even though it means putting a family of two, three, four, or five into one room. But this is better than putting two or three families in a single tent."[74]

In August 1950, Meir also developed a massive public works program to create jobs for the unemployed. Meir's plan centered on building a system of roads throughout Israel. Her critics complained that Israel needed more industry and more agriculture before it developed new roads and that by wanting to do everything at once Meir was trying to bankrupt the new country. Meir felt that the road program

Meir worked to improve conditions for Israeli soldiers and immigrants during her stint as Israel's minister of labor.

was vital for the country, however, and deserved equal priority with industrial projects and increasing agricultural sites.

To her critics, Meir responded, "If we have to choose between making a road or vegetable-growing," she said, "I'm for vegetables. If we have to choose between a road and clearing land for cultivation—then clearing the land, definitely. If we have to choose between a road and planning new orange groves—I'm for new orange groves. But the upshot is that we haven't one or the other." [75]

Meir won again. The roads were built and became known in Hebrew as *goldene wegen*, or golden roads. Meir's plans were not always popular, especially with the Ministry of Finance, with which she battled constantly for funds for her projects. But more often than not Meir put her programs into action. She loved working in the Ministry of Labor and felt like she had found the perfect place for her talents. But in 1956, Meir was once again forced to make a career

change when the prime minister appointed her as Israel's foreign minister.

Meir made her feelings about the appointment clear when she heard the news: "What does Ben-Gurion want with me? All a foreign minister does is talk and talk more. One day this way, another day that way. . . . Here at the labor ministry, at least I can make a house, I can build a road, or get a law passed. I do something and I can see it with my own eyes. . . . In the foreign ministry all they do is talk." [76]

Foreign Minister

But once again Ben-Gurion prevailed, and in June 1956 Meir changed offices. Her first act as foreign minister was to change her name from Meyerson to Meir, following orders from Ben-Gurion that all foreign service personnel assume the Hebrew version of their names. The choice of a

Meir's aggressive development plans often drew criticism that she was trying to do too much too soon.

An Israeli tank maneuvers into Egypt during the Suez-Sinai War. During the short war, Israeli forces seized the Sinai peninsula and the Gaza Strip.

new last name would prove to be one of the easiest decisions Meir had to make during her tenure as foreign minister.

Meir came to her new post at a time of increasing international tension and a growing threat of war. The last British soldiers were pulling out of Egypt, and the Soviet Union was stepping up the sale of arms to Israel's Arab neighbors. Shortly after taking office, Meir was faced with her first international crisis. The emergency began in July 1956 when Egypt "nationalized" (i.e., seized) the Suez Canal and blocked the passage of many international vessels, including all Israeli ships. In the months that followed, Egypt, Syria, and Jordan unified their military commands and began calling for the downfall of Israel. War was imminent. Israeli leaders decided the country's survival depended on a first strike. In conjunction with France and Great Britain, both countries with major financial investments in the canal, Israel made plans to liberate the canal zone.

The Suez-Sinai War

The Israeli forces struck with lightning swiftness on October 29, 1956. In less than four days, Israeli forces seized the entire Sinai peninsula, bordering the Gulf of Suez in northeastern Egypt, and all of the Gaza Strip, the coastal strip on the Egyptian-Israeli border. During the short war, in which Israeli soldiers claimed land three times the size of Israel, 172 Israeli soldiers were killed and 800 wounded.

Once their defeat was a certainty, the surrounding Arab states lodged protests with the United Nations. A UN Emergency Force was sent to supervise a cease-fire in the region. As soon as the UN forces were in place, the Arab nations appealed to the United Nations for the return of their land. Following the Arab request, the United Nations passed a resolution that Israel, Britain, and France withdraw from all areas they had occupied during the war. In

A Shared History

Golda firmly believed that Africa and Israel had similar histories. She felt that Israel and the emerging African nations could work together for the benefit of both. In her autobiography, Golda wrote of African persecution.

"There is still one other question arising out of the disaster of the nations which remains unsolved to this day, and whose profound tragedy only a Jew can comprehend. This is the African question. Just call to mind all of those terrible episodes of the slave trade, of human beings who, merely because they were black, were stolen like cattle, taken prisoner, captured and sold. Their children grew up in strange lands, the objects of contempt and hostility because their complexions were different. I am not ashamed to say, though I may expose myself to ridicule in saying so, that once I have witnessed the redemption of the Jews, my people, I wish also to assist in the redemption of the Africans."

Meir believed that Africans and Jews shared a common history of persecution.

a rare instance of cooperation, the United States and the Soviet Union both supported the UN resolution.

France and Britain both agreed to the terms outlined in the resolution, but Israel resisted. The Israeli government demanded control of two border areas that had become bases for Arab strikes prior to the war. Finally, bending to UN pressure, Israel agreed to withdraw if the United Nations would replace Israeli troops with a UN peacekeeping force. As foreign minister, Meir formally accepted the UN demands: "The Government of Israel is now in a position to announce its plans for full and prompt withdrawal from the Sharm el-Sheikh area, and the Gaza Strip."[77] Making this statement, and then watching the Egyptian army sweep back into the area and release all Arab prisoners held on charges of terrorism, was one of the low points in Meir's life. Israel had fought and won a decisive war, but had gained nothing. Once again those who sought Israel's destruction were free to establish military posts directly across the border from Israel. In her autobiography, Meir recorded her feelings that day: "The Egyptian military government, with its garrison, was going to return to Gaza. There was nothing I could do or say. . . . It was not one of the finest moments of my life."[78]

Though Meir considered this a dark period in her life, her tireless work won her staunch praise throughout the country. Prime Minister Ben-Gurion, whom Meir alternately battled and loudly defended during political meetings, often praised Meir as the only "man" in his cabinet, meaning that she was stronger and more outspoken than any of his other cabinet members.

Israel and Africa

Accepting treaties that she did not support and fighting political battles in the diplomatic arena rankled, but, while Meir disliked many of her responsibilities as foreign minister, one of the bright spots of her job as foreign minister was her work with African nations. In the winter of 1957, Meir attended an Afro-Asian conference in Tel Aviv. There she learned that the problems facing the emerging African nations were similar to those facing Israel during its first years. Remembering her happier days in the labor ministry, Meir decided this was an ideal project for her ministry.

In 1958 Meir made her first visit to Africa, and everywhere she went she spoke of Israel's willingness to help the emerging nations increase their skills in the areas of farming, education, land settlement, and community development. As part of her program, Meir sent thousands of Israeli engineers, teachers, doctors, agriculture specialists, and civil administrators to Africa to teach the emerging nations what Israel had learned. Meir's advice to those she sent was always "Tell them about the mistakes we made. So they won't repeat them."[79] Meir also hosted African political leaders, students, and teachers on inspection tours of the flourishing nation that had been built by the Jewish immigrants. Meir's program was a success and built strong bonds of Israeli-African friendship. African families named their children after her, and letters poured in from African nations praising her and her programs. In the 1970s, under the threat of an oil embargo from the Arab nations, many African nations expediently renounced their ties with Israel. But while Meir served as foreign minister, friendship

Golda dines with her son, Menachem, and his family. Meir had planned to retire in 1965 to live a quiet life and enjoy her role as a grandmother.

and cooperation between Israel and the countries of Africa blossomed.

Retiring from Public Life

As much as she loved the African program, the constant travel and the strain of international politics began to wear on Meir. She often appeared exhausted and was frequently ill, causing her friends to worry about her health. "I couldn't avoid coming to the conclusion that the responsibilities I had shouldered for more than thirty years were starting to weigh on me too heavily," Meir later wrote in her autobiography. "I didn't want to live forever, but also I didn't want to turn into a semi-invalid."[80]

In 1965, at the age of sixty-seven, Meir officially retired from public life and left Jerusalem to live in a small house in Tel

Aviv near her son, Menachem, and his wife, Aya. For a few months, Meir was wonderfully happy exploring her new role as grandmother and private citizen of Israel. But her peace and retirement were short-lived. The Labor Party, for which Meir had worked for so long, was being torn apart by internal power struggles. Huge rifts caused by personality conflicts between party leaders, differences between pro-Western and pro-Soviet delegates, and a worsening economic situation led friends within the government to beg Meir to return to public life as the secretary-general of the party and a generally mediating influence. And so, reluctantly, Meir returned. She explained:

It was the one appeal that I couldn't turn down. Not because I was so sure that I would succeed or because I so yearned to be in the middle of a crucial struggle all over again—and not because I was bored, as many people probably thought—but for a much simpler and much more important reason: I truly believed that the future of the labor movement was at stake. And although I could hardly bear the idea of giving up the peace and quiet I had

A Dream of Peace

In a 1969 address to the AFL-CIO convention in Atlantic City, Meir talked of her dream for peace in the Middle East. Even when her new nation was on the verge of war, Meir believed that Jews and Arabs would eventually live in peace. The following is excerpted from Peggy Mann's Golda.

"I believe that the first thing that is necessary for people in the world is the courage to dream great dreams, and then the reality to face difficulties in order to accomplish and make these dreams come true. And I believe in this as sincerely as I believe that the day must come when there will be real peace between us and the Arabs. I have said over and over again I do not believe, I refuse to believe, that Egyptian mothers in the Nile Valley are giving birth to their children and have them for the great and glorious ideal that when their boy reaches the age of eighteen or seventeen or nineteen, he will go off to war and fight the Israelis and who knows whether he will come back. But maybe he will be very successful in killing the son of a Jewish mother in Israel. I do not believe that this is what Egyptian mothers are giving birth to their children for. I do not believe that Egyptian and Syrian and Iraqi and Jordanian mothers are prepared to see their infants die because of lack of medical care, and just for the great future that lies before them—maybe they will finally succeed in killing the children of Israeli mothers. I refuse to believe it.

Once their leaders realize this and once the masses among the Arab people dare to stand up and say to their leaders, 'There is no glory in having our sons killed. We gave birth to them in order that they may be alive,' I see a future for friendship, peace, cooperation between our neighbors and ourselves. . . . It will be a great day when the young Jew from this side of the Jordan on his farm will cross the Jordan not with tanks, not with planes, but with tractors and with a hand of friendship as between farmer and farmer, as human being and human being. A dream? Maybe. I am sure it will come true."

finally attained—even if for only a few months—I couldn't turn my back at this stage of my life either on my principles or on my colleagues. So I said yes and went back to work, to traveling, to incessant meetings and to the bondage of an appointment book, but I promised myself—and my children—that this was the last job I would ever do.[81]

Meir proved to be a stabilizing force in the Labor Party, and the rifts began to heal. Meir was one of a few people who members of all factions trusted, and she had already attained international acclaim through her past service in the government. Many considered Meir the perfect candidate to fill the office of prime minister when Levi Eshkol died on February 26, 1969. It seemed a logical choice to everyone but Meir, who was stunned when the Israeli cabinet named her as their choice for prime minister. At first seventy-year-old Meir refused, citing her age and ill health. But party leaders pressed her to at least serve as interim prime minister until elections could be held in October. Once again called to duty, Meir accepted.

On March 7, 1969, the Central Committee of the Labor Party officially nominated Meir as prime minister. Meir later recorded her feelings on that day:

I have often been asked how I felt at that moment, and I wish that I had a poetic answer to the question. I know that tears rolled down my cheeks and that I held my head in my hands when the voting was over, but all that I recall about my feelings is that I was dazed. I had never planned to be prime minister; I had never planned any position, in fact . . . I only knew that now I would have to make decisions every day that would affect the lives of millions of people, and I think perhaps that is why I cried.[82]

8 Prime Minister Meir

Meir's term as prime minister was not an easy one. She took office on the heels of one war and stepped down five years later at the close of another. The period of her leadership was one of high tension in the Middle East, during which Israel was constantly in a state of alert. Much hostility concerned the disputed territory that Israel claimed in what came to be known as the Six-Day War.

The Six-Day War began on June 5, 1967, when Israel launched preemptive air strikes against Egyptian airfields and Egyptian, Syrian, and Jordanian armies massed on its borders. Israel, against all expectations, won the war. Within the first six hours, Israeli bombs disabled four hundred aircraft in Egypt, Syria, and Jordan, effectively destroying Arab air power. Within six days, Israeli forces had defeated the three enemy armies and swept back into the lands they had taken, and later returned, during the Suez-Sinai War.

Further Conflict

The conflict left Israel in possession of the Gaza Strip and the vast Sinai peninsula to the south, all of Jerusalem, the West Bank of the Jordan River, and the Golan Heights in the north separating Israel and Syria. At the close of the war, Israeli leaders vowed that they would not withdraw from these territories until a peace treaty could be negotiated with surrounding Arab countries. At the time, Meir was confident that peace in the Middle East was assured. She wrote of her feelings about the war:

> There may still be people who do not understand that we fought that war so successfully not only because we were made to fight it, but also because we most profoundly hoped that we would achieve a victory so complete that we would never have to fight again. If the defeat of the Arab armies massed against us could be made total, then perhaps our neighbors would finally give up their "holy war" against us and realize that peace was as necessary for them as for us and that the lives of their sons were as precious as the lives of our sons.[83]

But instead of ensuring peace, the war only led to further conflict. The occupied territories became a major political football both within Israel and on the international scene. Leaders of the Israeli Orthodox religious parties opposed withdrawal from the West Bank and Gaza. Even in Meir's Labor Party, opinion was divided. Some members wanted the land annexed

(Above) Soldiers scramble out of their transport during the Six-Day War.
(Below) A masked Palestinian sprays an anti-Semitic message on a wall.
Israeli seizure of Arab lands during the Six-Day War brought with it the
guarantee of continued unrest.

into Israel, others called for withdrawal, and some supported a partial withdrawal in which Israel would retain only areas vital to military security. Arab leaders and their allies called for an immediate unconditional withdrawal from the area and threatened oil embargoes against countries that retained ties to Israel.

The Israelis found themselves locked in a war with Arab terrorists who vowed to make the cost of living in Israel so high that all immigrants would leave. Israeli civilians and soldiers were victims of bombings at schools, temples, and public buildings, and Israeli diplomats were killed by letter bombs in embassy offices around the world. From *My Life:*

> We learned to hold out against the terror, to protect our aircraft and passengers, to turn our embassies into small fortresses and to patrol schoolyards

and city streets. I walked behind the coffins and visited the bereaved families of the victims of Arab terrorism, and I was filled with pride that I belonged to a nation that was able to take these blows—these cowardly and evil blows—without saying, "Enough. We have had enough. Give the terrorists whatever they want because we have taken all that we can take." Other governments surrendered to the demands of the terrorists, put planes at their disposal and released them from jail, while the foreign press and the New Left called them "guerrillas" and "freedom fighters." For us, however, they remained criminals, not heros.[84]

As prime minister, Meir found herself pressured both at home and abroad re- garding the occupied territories. Israeli citizens were crying for the annexation of the occupied territories and for an end to terrorist activities. At the same time, the United States was pressing Meir to negotiate a peace treaty with the Arabs that included withdrawal from the occupied territories.

Pressure from All Sides

During her first months in office, Meir made secret visits to world leaders in pursuit of peace in the Middle East. Meir also frequently reiterated her appeal to the Arab nations to meet with Israel for treaty negotiations, but her entreaties

"Each Land Must Decide"

In an address to the United Nations in 1970, Meir spoke of her desire to balance sovereignty and cooperation in the Middle East. The following passage is from Peggy Mann's Golda.

"I am convinced that all of us in the Middle East will continue to exist as sovereign states. None of us will leave. But we may choose whether we will continue in the sterile course of mutual destruction, whether we will go on hurting each other to no one's benefit, or whether we will venture on a constructive course and build our lands separately and together.

For each of us to attain the best for his people, cooperation with his neighbors in the solution of regional problems is essential. Our borders not only separate us but are bridges between us.

No people is an island. We are bound to each other by the problems of our region, our world. We can make of these ties a curse or a blessing. Each nation, each land must decide."

were ignored. Throughout this time, the terrorist raids increased along with pressure from the United States to withdraw from the occupied territories. Finally, Meir decided to go to the United States and personally plead Israel's case to President Richard Nixon. Not only was Israel not going to withdraw, Meir was determined to ask the United States for more arms for her country to defend itself:

> I had to lay before the President all our problems and difficulties, quite candidly, and try to convince him, beyond a shadow of doubt, that there was a great deal that could be asked of us by way of compromise and concessions, but that we could not be expected to give up our dream of peace or to withdraw a single soldier from one inch of land until an agreement could be reached between the Arabs and ourselves. And that was not all. We desperately needed arms, and I felt that I should ask him for them myself.[85]

Prime Minister Golda Meir poses with U.S. president Richard Nixon after their 1973 meeting. Although Nixon demanded that Israel withdraw from the occupied territories seized during the Six-Day War, Meir adamantly refused.

No Deals

Meir was appalled by any nation's concession to terrorist demands. Following Austria's decision to close an Israeli immigration center after threats from an Arab terrorist group, Meir gave the following speech, excerpted in My Life.

"It is a choice that every government must make these days. . . . *But there can be no deals with terrorism.* What has happened in Vienna is that, for the first time, a government has come to an understanding, an agreement, with the terrorists. A basic principle of freedom of movement of peoples has been put under question, at any rate for Jews, and this in itself is a great victory for terrorism and for terrorists. . . . If it has decided that rather than do away with terrorism, it will set terrorists free and give them whatever they ask for, then it will have raised the question of whether any country can permit itself to be involved in allowing Jews to use its soil for transit."

Meir's visit achieved partial success. She returned with no firm promises but with an informal understanding that the United States would give military aid to Israel. Although this was good news to the Israeli public, the need for arms was just one of many problems facing the country at the time.

Domestic Problems

In addition to the continual threat of war, the country faced high inflation, labor strikes, housing shortages, high unemployment, and a continuing flood of new immigrants. As a dedicated member of the Labor Party, Meir had always firmly believed in organized labor and the right of workers to strike for better wages or working conditions. But as prime minister, when the strikes threatened Israel's welfare, she found herself issuing orders that countered her basic beliefs. She wrote in her autobiography, "I don't think that I need to explain to anyone what it meant to me personally to have to decide on issuing restraining orders when the staffs of hospitals went on strike. But there was no other way to ensure that there wouldn't be a resultant loss of life, so I grit my teeth and did it."[86]

Meir devoted many hours to the domestic problems that plagued her country but spent the bulk of her time in pursuit of peace. Any hint that peace might be possible would send Meir into furious activity and keep her working in her office from dawn to the early hours of the following morning. For Meir peace was the most important prize to be won. Meir's dedication and determination won her both praise and criticism. One veteran diplomat who worked with Meir described her determination as one of her greatest strengths and greatest weaknesses. Meir doggedly

A man prays in the foreground while troops move through the desert during the 1973 Yom Kippur War.

defended her ideals and staunchly resisted all attempts to destroy her aims. These characteristics proved invaluable to the embattled Jews, but they impaired her ability to adapt to changing circumstances.

The Yom Kippur War

Meir's battle for peace in Israel was one of the few she would lose. On October 6, 1973, Syria and Egypt, frustrated by Israel's refusal to leave the occupied territories, launched a surprise attack on Israeli occupation forces. The war began on Yom Kip-

pur, the holiest of Jewish holidays, which is celebrated by family gatherings and religious services. In Israel most public services were suspended for the holiday, and as many soldiers as possible were given leave to be with their families.

The morning before the attack, reports reached Meir that Russian advisers and their families in Syria were hastily leaving the country. During the preceding week, reports had trickled in to Jerusalem of troop buildups in both Syria and Egypt. Troubled by these reports, Meir called an emergency meeting of those ministers who had remained in Jerusalem for the holidays. During the meeting, Meir's military and intelligence advisers asserted their belief that the buildup indicated normal Syrian maneuvers and not an imminent war. Still Meir was uneasy, writing later:

> Today I know what I should have done. I should have overcome my hesitations. I knew as well as anyone else what full-scale mobilization meant and how much money it would cost, and I also knew that only a few months before, in May, we had an alert and the reserves had been called up; but nothing had happened. But I also understood that perhaps there had been no war in May exactly because the reserves had been called up. That Friday morning I should have listened to the warning of my own heart and ordered a call up. For me, that fact cannot and never will be erased, and there can be no consolation in anything that anyone else has to say or in all of the common sense rationalizations with which my colleagues have tried to comfort me. . . . I will never again be the person I was before the Yom Kippur War.[87]

Meir went to bed that night troubled and uneasy. She was awakened at 4 A.M. by a call from her military secretary. Intelligence sources had discovered that Syrian and Egyptian troops were prepared to attack late that afternoon. After emergency cabinet meetings with her ministers, Meir issued a general call to all troops and also sent an urgent appeal to the United States for diplomatic help in stopping the Arab attack before it was launched. But there was no time for diplomatic solutions. The Arab armies launched their offensive shortly after noon, six hours earlier than anticipated.

Israel found itself fighting on two fronts at once as Syria attacked the Golan Heights and Egypt attacked troops in the Sinai. The initial reports from the front lines were grim; Israeli soldiers suffered heavy casualties and the Arab armies seemed to be sweeping into Israel. During the first day of the war, Meir went on Israeli television to address her shocked nation:

> We are in no doubt that we shall prevail. But we are also convinced that this renewal of Egyptian and Syrian aggression is an act of madness. We did our best to prevent the outbreak. We appealed to quarters with political influence to use it in order to frustrate this infamous move of the Egyptian and Syrian leaders. While there was still time we informed friendly countries of the confirmed information that we had of the plans for an offensive against Israel. We called on them to do their utmost to prevent war, but the Egyptian and Syrian attack has started.[88]

Foreign Aid

The Syrians, aided by troops from Jordan and Iraq, initially gained ground in the north and south, and the Egyptian army crossed the Suez Canal and penetrated about six miles into the Israeli-occupied Sinai before it was stopped. Some of Meir's advisers began talking about conditions of Israel's surrender, an idea that Meir refused to consider. Instead, Meir used all of her personal persuasion and years of political experience to bring pressure on her allies. It was time for Israel's friends to deliver on their promises. Meir issued pleas to both Secretary of State Henry Kissinger and President Nixon; the promised American weapons and supplies must be delivered immediately. Meir even offered to fly secretly to the United States to personally meet with the president, but that proved unnecessary: On October 14, U.S. cargo planes began arriving in Israel carrying armaments and much-needed supplies. In her autobiography, Meir wrote of the American assistance, "The airlift was invaluable. . . . When I heard that the planes had touched down . . . I cried for the first time since the war had begun, though not for the last. That was also the day on which we published the first casualty list—656 Israelis had already died in battle."[89]

With the additional arms and supplies, the Israeli army launched a successful counterattack. On October 16, the Israeli army broke through the opposing forces and swept into Egypt and fought the Syrian forces to a standstill. Finally, the United Nations stepped in and arranged a cease-fire between the warring nations. The cease-fire took effect on the Syrian front on October 22 and in Egypt two days later. Twenty-five hundred Israeli soldiers had been killed in the fighting. The war left Israelis deeply shaken. Most of the population felt that Meir's government had been caught napping. Meir wrote,

Jubilant members of an Israeli defense force celebrate after they stopped Syrian forces in the Sinai. Despite this victory, Israel would continue to be besieged by its neighbors.

Despite the growing feeling that perhaps this time the disengagement would grow into a real peace, the general mood in Israel was very black. From all sections of the population there came demands that the government resign, accusations that the army's poor state of preparedness was the result of faulty leadership, of complacency and of a total lack of communication between the government and the people.[90]

Protest against the government continued to grow. According to historian Robert Slater:

> The movement began among the soldiers, who were most aware of the state of unpreparedness in which [Israel] had found itself at the outbreak of war. They had been gradually returning from the fronts since November and December 1973. Now most of them were home, full of anguish and horror at what they had seen; a return to normal life seemed impossible to those who had witnessed the heaviest casualties in war for twenty-five years.[91]

Protesters chanted antigovernment slogans during public events and demanded an investigation into the country's unpreparedness for the devastating Yom Kippur War. One of Meir's most outspoken opponents was Menachem Begin, leader of the opposition party in the Knesset. Begin openly demanded Meir's resignation during Knesset debates. "Why did you not mobilize the reserves before Yom Kippur?" Begin demanded of Meir. "Why did you not move reinforcements to the fronts?. . . You may well say, blessed is the nation which has such soldiers to fight for

it. But you cannot say, blessed is the nation which has such a government to lead it!"[92]

A Terrible Wound

The Yom Kippur War left seventy-five-year-old Meir a changed woman. For the rest of her life she was haunted by the feeling that if only she had acted earlier fewer Israeli soldiers would have died. Exhausted and in ill health, Meir wanted to retire. Several times following the war, Meir quietly offered to resign her office, but the Labor Party rejected her offer. Meir agreed to serve as prime minister through the general elections to be held on December 31, 1973, sure that a new prime minister would be selected. But despite strong criticism of the Labor Party and Meir herself, she was reelected prime minister. In her autobiography, Meir wrote of her second election, "I was beginning to feel the physical and psychological effects of the draining past few months. I was dead tired and not at all sure that, in this kind of situation, I could ever succeed in forming a government—or even whether I should go on trying to do so. . . . I felt I couldn't go on, and I told the party that I had had enough. But I was bombarded by delegations imploring me to change my mind."[93]

An official board of inquiry was charged with investigating Israel's lack of preparedness for the Yom Kippur War. Its preliminary report, issued on April 2, 1974, cleared Meir of any direct responsibility for the situation. The commission found that Meir had "decided wisely, with common sense and speedily, in favor of the full mobilization of the reserves, as recommended by the chief of staff despite weighty political considerations, thereby performing a most important service for the defense of the state."[94] Nevertheless, Meir held herself responsible.

Though officially exonerated, the seventy-six-year-old prime minister was tired, tired of fighting Israel's enemies and tired of fighting a battle for political unity inside her country. On April 10, 1974, Meir announced her resignation to the Labor Party. "Five years are sufficient. It is beyond my strength to continue carrying this burden. I don't belong to any circle or faction within the party. I have only a circle of one to consult—myself. And this time my decision is final, irrevocable. I beg of you not to try to persuade me to change my mind for any reason at all. It will not help."[95]

Meir insisted that her political career was over, although she remained in office until a new coalition government could be formed. Meir officially left office on June 4, 1974; one of her last announcements was of the successful negotiation of a disengagement treaty with Syria. The treaty was signed on June 5, 1974.

The Closing of an Era

For the remaining four years of her life, Meir led a quiet but still political life. Foreign dignitaries always called on her when they came to Israel, and a stream of politicians and statesmen continued to pay their respects. But Meir never officially returned to the political arena again. She died in Jerusalem on December 8, 1978, at last succumbing to the cancer she had been battling for fifteen years. Not even her closest friends knew of her illness, and the nation was shocked by her death. Meir re-

quested a simple funeral with no eulogies. But though her family honored her wishes, no one could stop the steady stream of mourners. Nearly one hundred thousand people lined up in front of the Knesset building to hear the brief funeral ceremony. The funeral was attended by dignitaries from around the world including former British prime minister Harold Wilson; Lillian Carter, mother of U.S. president Jimmy Carter; U.S. secretary of state Cyrus Vance; and former secretary of state Henry Kissinger.

In her autobiography, Meir wrote:

So to those who ask, "What of the future?" I still have only one answer: I believe that we will have peace with our neighbors, but I am sure that no one

Meir wanted to retire from her post as prime minister immediately after the Yom Kippur War. She left office in 1974.

Crowds flock to Golda Meir's grave to show respect for the deceased leader. Meir's dream for a peaceful homeland remains unachieved.

will make peace with a weak Israel. If Israel is not strong, there will be no peace.

My vision for the future? A Jewish state in which masses of Jews from all over the world will continue to settle and to build; an Israel bound in a collaborative effort with its neighbors on behalf of all the people in the region; an Israel that remains a flourishing democracy and a society resting firmly on social justice and equality.[96]

Throughout her life, Meir dreamed of a time when Israel and her Arab neighbors could live in peace and prosperity. That day has not yet arrived, though the peace process continues in fits and starts. In 1979, Israel and Egypt signed a peace treaty. And in September 1993 Israeli prime minister Yitzhak Rabin and Palestine Liberation Organization leader Yasir Arafat made history when they signed an unprecedented accord. Nearly a year later, on July 25, 1994, Jordan and Israel officially ended a forty-six-year state of war when Jordan's King Hussein and Prime Minister Rabin signed a peace treaty.

Israel and her Arab neighbors still must resolve numerous differences; the peace Meir dreamed of has not yet come to pass. But with each new treaty, the country takes another step toward making Meir's dreams a reality.

Notes

Introduction: A Woman of Deep Convictions

1. Golda Meir, *My Life*. New York: G. P. Putnam's Sons, 1975, p. 379.

2. Quoted in Israel and Mary Shenker, *As Good as Golda: The Warmth and Wisdom of Israel's Prime Minister*. New York: McCall, 1970, p. 5.

Chapter 1: The Shaping of a Revolutionary

3. Meir, *My Life*, p. 13.

4. Meir, *My Life*, p. 14.

5. Meir, *My Life*, p. 13.

6. Quoted in Ralph G. Martin, *Golda Meir: The Romantic Years*. New York: Charles Scribner's Sons, 1988, p. 7.

7. Quoted in David Goldberg and John Rayner, *The Jewish People: Their Story and Their Religion*. New York: Viking Penguin, 1987, p. 186.

8. Meir, *My Life*, p. 21.

9. Quoted in Martin, *Golda Meir*, p. 12.

10. Quoted in Martin, *Golda Meir*, p. 18.

Chapter 2: A Taste of Freedom

11. Meir, *My Life*, p. 30.

12. Meir, *My Life*, p. 30.

13. Quoted in Meir, *My Life*, p. 31.

14. Quoted in Karen McAuley, *Golda Meir*. New York: Chelsea House, 1985, p. 24.

15. Quoted in Martin, *Golda Meir*, p. 25.

16. Meir, *My Life*, p. 34.

17. Quoted in Martin, *Golda Meir*, p. 29.

18. Quoted in Martin, *Golda Meir*, p. 33.

19. Quoted in Martin, *Golda Meir*, p. 33.

20. Quoted in Martin, *Golda Meir*, p. 33.

21. Quoted in Martin, *Golda Meir*, p. 37.

22. Quoted in Martin, *Golda Meir*, p. 38.

23. Quoted in Martin, *Golda Meir*, p. 39.

24. Quoted in Martin, *Golda Meir*, p. 39.

Chapter 3: Educating a Rebel

25. Meir, *My Life*.

26. Meir, *My Life*, p. 46.

27. Meir, *My Life*, p. 50.

28. Quoted in Martin, *Golda Meir*, p. 47.

29. Meir, *My Life*, p. 50.

30. Meir, *My Life*, p. 52.

31. Quoted in Martin, *Golda Meir*, p. 63.

32. Meir, *My Life*, p. 54.

33. Quoted in Martin, *Golda Meir*, p. 67.

34. Meir, *My Life*, p. 63.

35. Meir, *My Life*, p. 63.

Chapter 4: To Palestine

36. David Ben-Gurion, *Israel: A Personal History*. New York: Sabra Books, 1971, p. 41.

37. Quoted in Amos Perlmutter, *Israel: The Partitioned State: A Political History Since 1900*. New York: Charles Scribner's Sons, 1985, p. 25.

38. Quoted in Meir, *My Life*, p. 68.

39. Meir, *My Life*, p. 67.

40. Quoted in Martin, *Golda Meir*, p. 87.

41. Quoted in Terry Morris, *Shalom Golda*. New York: Hawthorn Books, 1971.

42. Meir, *My Life*, p. 75.

Chapter 5: Building a New Life

43. Meir, *My Life*, p. 80.

44. Meir, *My Life*.

45. Quoted in Martin, *Golda Meir*, p. 121.

46. Meir, *My Life*, p. 97.

47. Meir, *My Life*, p. 100.

48. Quoted in Peggy Mann, *Golda: The Life of Israel's Prime Minister*. New York: Coward, McCann, and Geoghegan, 1971, p. 138.

49. Meir, *My Life*, p. 114.

50. Quoted in Martin, *Golda Meir*, p. 148.

51. Quoted in Mann, *Golda*, p. 71.

52. Meir, *My Life*, p. 115.

Chapter 6: The Birth of a Nation

53. Quoted in Robert Slater, *Golda: The Uncrowned Queen of Israel*. Middle Village, NY: Jonathan David, 1981, p. 43.

54. Perlmutter, *Israel: The Partitioned State*, p. 54.

55. Quoted in Ronald Sanders, *The High Walls of Jerusalem: A History of the Balfour Declaration and the Birth of the British Mandate for Palestine*. New York: Holt, Rinehart and Winston, 1983, p. 664.

56. Meir, *My Life*, p. 179.

57. Quoted in Conor Cruise O'Brien, *The Siege: The Saga of Israel and Zionism*. New York: Simon and Schuster, 1986, p. 241.

58. Meir, *My Life*, p. 164.

59. Meir, *My Life*, p. 182.

60. Meir, *My Life*, p. 200.

61. Meir, *My Life*, p. 191.

62. Quoted in Mann, *Golda*, p. 157.

63. Quoted in O'Brien, *The Siege*, p. 272.

64. Meir, *My Life*, p. 213.

65. Meir, *My Life*, p. 226.

66. Quoted in Martin, *Golda Meir*, p. 342.

67. Quoted in Martin, *Golda Meir*, p. 343.

68. Meir, *My Life*, p. 234.

Chapter 7: Political Years

69. Meir, *My Life*, p. 236.

70. Quoted in Mann, *Golda*, p. 169.

71. Quoted in Mann, *Golda*, p. 170.

72. Quoted in Slater, *Golda*, p. 89.

73. Quoted in Mann, *Golda*, p. 177.

74. Quoted in Slater, *Golda*, p. 98.

75. Quoted in Slater, *Golda*, p. 99.

76. Quoted in Slater, *Golda*, p. 118.

77. Quoted in Mann, *Golda*, p. 197.

78. Meir, *My Life*, p. 308.

79. Quoted in Mann, *Golda*, p. 200.

80. Meir, *My Life*, p. 347.

81. Meir, *My Life*, p. 352.

82. Meir, *My Life*, p. 379.

Chapter 8: Prime Minister Meir

83. Meir, *My Life*, p. 364.

84. Meir, *My Life*, p. 399.

85. Meir, *My Life*, p. 387.

86. Meir, *My Life*, p. 397.

87. Meir, *My Life*, p. 425.

88. Quoted in Slater, *Golda*, p. 241.

89. Meir, *My Life*, p. 431.

90. Meir, *My Life*, p. 449.

91. Robert Slater, *Rabin of Israel*. New York: St. Martin's Press, 1993, p. 203.

92. Quoted in Eric Silver, *Begin: The Haunted Prophet*. New York: Random House, 1984, p. 146.

93. Meir, *My Life*, p. 455.

94. Quoted in Meir, *My Life*, p. 452.

95. Meir, *My Life*, p. 458.

96. Meir, *My Life*, p. 460.

For Further Reading

David Ben-Gurion, *Israel: Years of Challenge*. New York: Holt, Rinehart and Winston, 1963. A history of the development of Israel as seen through the eyes of a key participant.

Larry Collins and Dominique Lapierre, *O Jerusalem!* New York: Simon and Schuster, 1972. Novelization of the birth of Israel, based on participants' personal narratives.

Mollie Keller, *Golda Meir*. New York: Franklin Watts, 1983. A juvenile biography that examines Meir's life and impact on Israel.

Nadav Safran, *From War to War: The Arab-Israeli Confrontation, 1948–1967*. New York: Pegasus, 1968. A survey of Israeli wars since statehood.

Leonard Stein, *The Balfour Declaration*. New York: Simon and Schuster, 1961. A history of the British Mandate to support a Jewish homeland in Palestine.

Works Consulted

Yossi Beilin, *Israel: A Concise Political History*. New York: St. Martin's Press, 1992. A historical review of the Zionist movement. Looks at the economic and political milestones that led to the founding of Israel.

David Ben-Gurion, *Israel: A Personal History*. New York: Sabra Books, 1971. A personal account of the history of Israel told by a leader of the Zionist movement and one of the founders of Israel.

Nicholas Bethell, *The Palestine Triangle: The Struggle for the Holy Land, 1935–48*. New York: G. P. Putnam's Sons, 1979. A historical look at the struggle for Palestine and a close look at the last years of the British Mandate.

Trevor Dupuy, *Elusive Victory: The Arab-Israeli Wars 1947–1974*. New York: Harper & Row, 1978. A military history and political analysis of the personnel, arms, strategies, and maneuvers of modern Middle East conflict.

Abba Eban, *Voice of Israel*. New York: Horizon Press, 1957. An Israeli politician's account of the formative history of Israel.

Simha Flappan, *The Birth of Israel: Myths and Realities*. New York: Random House, 1987. Social history examining widely perceived ideas of Israeli history and delving beneath the myth to reveal hidden truths.

David Goldberg and John Rayner, *The Jewish People: Their Story and Their Religion*. New York: Viking Penguin, 1987. A general history of the Jews from a religious viewpoint.

Walter Laqueur, *A History of Zionism*. New York: Schocken, 1989. The history of Zionism from the late 1800s through the early 1950s. Also probes the role of Zionism in world history.

Peggy Mann, *Golda: The Life of Israel's Prime Minister*. New York: Coward, McCann, and Geoghegan, 1971. A juvenile biography of Golda Meir.

Ralph G. Martin, *Golda Meir: The Romantic Years*. New York: Charles Scribner's Sons, 1988. A biography focusing on the social and personal life of Golda Meir. Also examines the personal price Meir paid for her political power.

Karen McAuley, *Golda Meir*. New York: Chelsea House, 1985. A good general biography.

Golda Meir, *My Life*. New York: G. P. Putnam's Sons, 1975. Meir's autobiography; revealing personal insights into her life and political career.

Menachem Meir, *My Mother Golda Meir*. New York: Arbor House, 1983. An affectionate biography of Meir written by her son.

Terry Morris, *Shalom Golda*. New York: Hawthorn Books, 1971. A portrayal of Meir's life and the challenges she faced both as a child and an adult. Includes comments obtained from Meir during interviews with the author.

Israel T. Naamani, *Israel: A Profile*. New York: Praeger, 1972. Surveys the geography and limited natural assets of the land. Also gives an overview of Jewish history.

Conor Cruise O'Brien, *The Siege: The Saga of Israel and Zionism*. New York: Simon and Schuster, 1986. Political history that explores the world events that led to the establishment of Israel. Opens with the waves of anti-Semitic violence that swept through eastern Europe at the end of the nineteenth century and continues through the Yom Kippur War.

Amos Perlmutter, *Israel: The Partitioned State: A Political History Since 1900*. New York: Charles Scribner's Sons, 1985. A general history of the twentieth-century development of the State of Israel.

Howard M. Sachar, *The Course of Modern Jewish History*. New York: Vintage Books, 1990. An encyclopedic history of Jews. Chronicles the history of the Jewish people and examines their impact on the modern world.

Ronald Sanders, *The High Walls of Jerusalem: A History of the Balfour Declaration and the Birth of the British Mandate for Palestine*. New York: Holt, Rinehart and Winston, 1983. Historical account of the events leading to the Balfour Declaration and its immediate import for the Zionist aspiration for a Jewish homeland.

Tom Segev, *1949: The First Israelis*. New York: Free Press, 1986. A history of the days leading up to and immediately following Israel's independence, written by one of Israel's leading journalists.

Israel and Mary Shenker, *As Good as Golda: The Warmth and Wisdom of Israel's Prime Minister*. New York: McCall, 1970. A compilation of Meir's quotations.

Eric Silver, *Begin: The Haunted Prophet*. New York: Random House, 1984. A comprehensive account of the events that shaped the life of the former Israeli leader and the influence he had on his nation and people.

Robert Slater, *Golda: The Uncrowned Queen of Israel*. Middle Village, NY: Jonathan David, 1981. A pictorial biography written by a leading American journalist living in Israel.

———, *Rabin of Israel*. New York: St. Martin's Press, 1993. A biography of Yitzhak Rabin, the first Israeli-born prime minister of Israel.

Index

Credits

Photos

Cover photo: AP/Wide World Photos

AP/Wide World Photos, 26, 32, 43, 77

Archive Photos/Express Newspapers, 96

Archive Photos, 29, 75, 82

Archive Photos/Jim Wells, 90

© ASAP/G.P.O./Woodfin Camp & Associates, Inc., 45, 50, 53, 69, 79, 80, 97

© ASAP/David Rubinger/Woodfin Camp & Associates, Inc., 9, 20, 57, 60, 65, 73, 84, 92, 94

The Bettmann Archive, 12, 14, 16, 36, 40

© Central Zionist Archive/ASAP/Woodfin Camp & Associates, Inc., 18

Corbis-Bettmann, 23

© Bernard Gotfryd/Woodfin Camp & Associates, Inc., 17

Library of Congress, 64

National Archives, 39, 63, 67

Reuters/Bettmann, 88 (bottom)

Sipa Press/Woodfin Camp & Associates, Inc., 88 (top)

Stock Montage, Inc., 24, 51

UPI/Corbis-Bettmann, 44, 54, 66, 81

Text

Quotations from *My Life* by Golda Meir are reprinted by permission of The Putnam Publishing Group (U.S.) and Weidenfeld Nicolson Ltd. (Canada). Copyright © 1975 by Golda Meir.

About the Author

Deborah Hitzeroth is a Virginia-based writer with a background in journalism and travel. Her background includes a Bachelor of Journalism degree from the University of Missouri and five years in print journalism as a reporter and editor. Following a brief stint as a section editor in California, she worked as a freelance writer for a monthly medical magazine in New York. This is her eighth book.